The Oval Office:
A Four-Time Olympian's Guide to Professional Track & Field
Copyright © 2019 by Lauryn C. Williams

Requests for information should be addressed to: contact@the-oval-office.com

Cover Design/Exterior: Robert Schwendenmann (bobbyhere@gmail.com)
Interior Layout/Formatting: Robert Schwendenmann
Editor: Sarah Wind

ISBN-10: 978-1-7327188-0-7
ISBN-13: 1-7327188-0-6

THE
OVAL
OFFICE

A FOUR-TIME OLYMPIAN'S GUIDE
TO PROFESSIONAL TRACK & FIELD

LAURYN C. WILLIAMS

This book is dedicated to my dad, David Williams,
who taught me the art of being resourceful and how to
show up and perform at critical moments.

And to everyone who ever ran a 400m race, you are my heroes.

TABLE OF CONTENTS

ACKNOWLEDGEMENTS

Writing doesn't come naturally to me. The journey this book has taken me on has been unbelievable to say the least. This has truly been a labor of love. I'd like to start by acknowledging the grind and thanking those who encouraged me when I wanted to quit.

I am grateful to all that read and critiqued the drafts: Ann Gaffigan, Wallace Spearmon Jr., Beth Mignano, Susan O'Connor, and my mommy. Susan Hazzard didn't bat an eye when I said I needed her help, and over Christmas break no less. Ato Boldon (who I convinced to sit still for three hours, not once but twice) made sure that the content was tip top. Bobby Schwendenmann managed this project until the end, and Sarah Wind was an editing angel sent from God. Special thanks to Brad Yewer who contributed advice from an agent's perspective, and to Dr. Wilhelm Lubbe for his patience and endless support.

To the world class, professional athletes who were so generous with their input:

- Brad Walker, IAAF World Championships gold medalist, pole vault
- Bernard Lagat, Olympic bronze and silver medalist, 1500m
- Amber Campbell, three-time Olympian, hammer throw
- Wallace Spearmon Jr., two-time Olympian, IAAF World Championships silver medalist (200m) and gold medalist (4x100 relay)
- Tiombe Hurd, American record holder, women's triple jump
- T'erea Brown, Olympian, 400 hurdles
- Matt Hemmingway, Olympic silver medalist, high jump

Everyone donated their time with the expectation that the return on investment would be helping the next generation of track and field athletes.

To all who helped me create the many memories throughout my career that shaped the content of this book, thank you.

PREFACE

In 2004, I was in my junior year of college, twenty years old and working my butt off to win the NCAA title in the 100m. I felt many times in the past that I was the best sprinter in the race, but somehow had never managed to make it to the finish line first. Professional track and field was not an aspiration for me. All I wanted to do was win college nationals.

When race day came, I was ready... and...I won. Not only did I win, but my time happened to be the second fastest time in the world that year. It was 2004, which was an Olympic year, and I was currently the fastest American woman. It was just weeks before the Olympic Trials. My life was about to change drastically.

Shortly after nationals, my coach sat me down and explained that though it was her job to build a great university team, she wouldn't be doing what was in my best interest if she didn't explain the opportunity that was now available to me. Yes, I could stay in school another year, but I would be taking a chance. The choice was up to me and I had several things to consider:

- What if I get injured?
- What if next year I am not as fast as I am now?
- What about my teammates? Am I ready to leave them behind?

After some reflection, I came to the conclusion that it was best to forego the remainder of my NCAA eligibility at the University of Miami and pursue my sports career. I was not old enough to drink or rent a car without paying an extra fee, but there I was making plans for a career as a professional athlete.

And so it started.

Time was of the essence and decisions needed to be made. I went from never really thinking about going pro to constantly pondering the best scenario. I could accept sponsorship money from a shoe company immediately which would have been the most conservative approach. I could wait to see how the Olympic Trials went. A good performance meant more bargaining power, but a poor one might damage the offer that was previously on the table. Maybe the smart decision would be for me to wait until after I made the team, and if I truly believed in myself I could wait until after the Olympic Games. Each option presented an opportunity to negotiate, but the more time I allowed to pass, the more substantial the risk.

Ultimately, I chose to become a professional right after the Olympic Trials which worked out well for me. I was fortunate (and grateful) to have my college coach to guide me through that process. Many young athletes are left to figure it out all alone. Some athletes' parents are involved in the decision-making process, but mine were not. They cheered for me, but they didn't have the slightest idea about the concept of going pro, going to the Olympics, making money from running, or having a career in track and field. They were focused on the free education! As long as that was achieved everything else was a bonus.

My story isn't unusual in the sense that most people have no idea where to start when transitioning from college to the professional ranks. There is a steep learning curve for parents and athletes who are faced with this option. It is hard to prepare for, whether opportunity knocks in the middle or at the end of your college years.

The key to having a successful career will hinge on your ability to learn everything you can, build a team of people you can trust, and commit to figuring a lot out along the way. You are embarking on a journey that 95% of the population, including your teammates, will probably never have to consider.

During my career I learned many lessons; some were difficult to endure. However I had a successful career as a professional that lasted ten years. I made the IAAF World Championships team five times and earned five medals. I was on four Olympic teams and managed to become the first American woman to earn a medal in the Summer and Winter Olympics.

I also embarked on the journey of finding new passions and meaningful work outside of sports. I earned my Finance degree, got my master's degree while competing, and then decided to become a CERTIFIED FINANCIAL PLANNER™ professional. I now run my own company where I help athletes organize their finances to make the most of their earnings. I love being part of their support team to help them make good choices.

I wish I had a resource to refer to while navigating the world of professional track and field to help me avoid some of the pitfalls I experienced. Track gave me so much to be thankful for and provided many skills I will use for the rest of my life. Though I am done competing, I want to continue to give back to the sport that has given so much to me. This book is my best effort at creating the "road map" I wish I would have had during my career. The objective advice you will find in these pages can be hard to obtain anywhere else. It is my pleasure to provide it and put it all in one place for you.

Welcome to the world of professional track and field.

INTRODUCTION

At the writing of this book a changing of the guard has just happened. My generation of track and field athletes is hanging up our spikes and the next generation has burst on the scene kicking butt and taking names. Some student-athletes are even going pro straight out of high school. Athletes from every track and field event are becoming household names because of the advancement of social media.

Unfortunately, the excitement of the being a professional athlete can quickly become stressful as you learn there are many responsibilities and decisions to be made, but no clear guidance on how to navigate the process. The opportunities are plentiful, but being strategic is key.

As a member of the veteran community making the mass exodus, I want to share as much of my experience with the next generation as possible. In this book, you will find useful, practical advice to aid you in the pursuit of your dream to become a professional athlete.

Track and field is much more than showing up and competing. If you want to be successful at the pro level you will have to embrace entrepreneurship. If you have no interest in running a business, then professional sports is not for you. I enjoyed a long career as a professional athlete. Having participated in four Olympic Games (2004, 2008, 2012, 2014), one of which was a Winter Olympics, I have definitely been around the track a few times. My experiences, both good and bad, are vast and varied. I have tried to keep the editorializing to a minimum in this book, and instead share real events and experiences to offer you the best chance at success. I will not sugarcoat the tough reality of professional sports or leave out the good parts, because there are many good parts.

Additionally, because I only competed in one discipline, I enlisted the help of some other Olympic athletes to make sure I captured various points of view. Please take the time to check out the acknowledgments page to learn more about who they are. They are greats in their respective events and their contributions add much value to the contents of this book.

This book uncovers and decodes the unwritten rules of being a successful professional athlete. It is designed primarily for track and field athletes new to the post-collegiate scene and that is why I write as if I am speaking directly to them. However parents, coaches, agents and other members of an athlete's support team should also find it helpful.I expect it to be enjoyable for fans who want to know more about how the sport works as well.

The more people are educated about the process of becoming an elite professional athlete, the better the overall track and field community will be. Coaches, you will learn how to set your athletes up to have the best experience possible. Parents, you will learn how to support your child as they navigate this process. Aspiring athletes, you will get best practices for choosing an agent and negotiating contracts.

Everyone's experience will be unique. Your path and my path to becoming a professional athlete will have similarities, but they will not be the same. My desire is to share all the tricks of the trade I have learned along the way, so you can avoid some of the common pitfalls and understand the secrets to a well-managed career. I aim to give you information about the options available so you can make an educated decision about your future. It is your future after all.

CHAPTER 1

WHAT IS A PROFESSIONAL?

"Professionalism is showing up. Every. Single. Day. It is commitment to this monotony, regardless of its discomfort. It is commitment to perseverance, to working hard, pushing ourselves outside of our comfort zones, over and over, accepting that there are no guarantees, and showing up anyway."

-*Stuart McMillan, CEO-ALTIS*

Though a noun by definition, the word *professional* is defined many ways. Merriam-Webster online defines professionalism as: participating for gain or livelihood in an activity or field of endeavor; exhibiting a courteous, conscientious, and generally businesslike manner in the workplace.

Being a professional is a mindset. It is an expected set of values and standards rooted in leadership and responsibility. In the rest of this chapter you will find some of the attributes of what it means to be a professional.

A Professional Is Compensated For Their Work

In track and field many athletes want to carry the title of "professional," and because there is no set criteria on what makes one a professional, the term is used very loosely. Simply competing on the next level after college doesn't automatically make you a pro. A professional does not just earn an income but also *makes a living from what they do*. There is a distinct difference.

Making a living consists of competing at a high level, winning competitions, and being paid. In this sport, the market for each event group is different and that means earning potential varies. Compensation comes from a variety of sources: endorsements (e.g. shoe and apparel contracts), prize money, and local sponsors. Your results on the track or the field affect your income. Your ranking affects your income. Your marks can affect your income. Your marketability affects your income.

Although competing and winning provide opportunities to earn more than enough to pay the bills, the world's best in a sport do not necessarily make the world's best money. Even earning a gold medal at the Olympic Games does not guarantee a life of fame and fortune. Many Olympic medalists find themselves searching for work months after winning big.

The secret is making the most of the opportunities that open up before you. There are many angles to maximize this potential, some of which you should be able to recognize and take advantage of, and others your agent will assist you with. Being a professional athlete requires you to possess and exhibit many qualities. These qualities can set you up for long-term financial success.

A Professional Is Focused On Their Business

Right now, you may be finishing your career as an NCAA All-American. You are probably thinking that being an All-American has to be good for some sort of contract that will provide smooth sailing financially. Unfortunately, that is not always the case.

When entering the world of professional track and field, forget that everything was done for you in college. There is no hand holding in the real world. As an athlete, it's all about business now. You are talented, but now everyone competing on this level is talented. Your talent won't organize your life or keep your schedule for you. Your attitude and approach will make or break you.

As alarming as it might seem, sponsors and agents are aware that athletes are business owners who don't know how to run a business. Instead of stepping in to equip them with skills to be better business owners, they will encourage athletes to outsource all the things that seem like too much to learn. An overwhelmed athlete is grateful for the person that swoops in and kindly takes care of everything for them. This is done in the name of focus and dedication, but there is a cost to this method.

Part of being a professional is having an understanding of the cash flow needed to keep the business running. Not every person who starts a business will understand the concept of fluctuating income. Yet, it is a part of entrepreneurship. It is also important to be realistic about what your physical body is capable of doing over the lifetime of your career. You only have so many performances in you, so you need to be selective about the number of times you compete. A professional does not get caught up in the moment but looks ahead and plans accordingly.

Consider this scenario. You just won a medal at the IAAF World Championships and with the prize money and some bonuses from your shoe sponsor, you walk away with $100,000. That's amazing. When you have been a starving college student for four years, $100,000 seems like a fortune. However, when will you be in this kind of race again? Will it be a year from now? Maybe two years? There are very slim odds that a person wins a race every time they are on the track, especially, the major championship. Now, that $100,000 doesn't seem like so much because it might be your only big pay day for quite awhile.

A professional values the help of someone with more expertise in a particular area, but a business owner understands the importance of learning the basic skills needed for personal success. A professional athlete is essentially a business owner who must be dedicated to developing in areas such as communications, scheduling, negotiating, planning, and relationship building.

A Professional Is a Good Communicator

Professionals know that communication is important. Consistent, open communication with your team is paramount. You are responsible for reading and responding to emails and voicemails! When your coach, sponsors, or USA Track and Field (USATF) contact you, do not blow them off. Pay attention to emails and voicemails, respond quickly to text messages, and know that quick communication will benefit you in the long run. If you are prompt at responding, you'll develop the reputation of being responsible and professional. You've heard that phrase "the early bird gets the worm," and in the business of track and field, a promptly returned phone call or email could mean an opportunity to expand your business.

In the age of social media, communication extends to the various social media platforms. You should be following relevant people and organizations on social media, which are covered in the Branding chapter. Entities will try to reach out to you and may choose to meet you on the platforms you are using regularly. It is not easy to keep track of different email accounts, text, voicemail, plus various messages sent through your social media accounts. However, in order to remain accessible and not miss an opportunity, you should check your social media accounts several times a week, if not daily.

Being up to date on the latest information about the sport is critical as a professional, whether that's competitions, anti-doping, or other rules. Know what the acronyms for different sports organizations stand for and what each organization is responsible for. Understanding these organizations' roles is crucial for your success as an athlete.

Professionals Show Good Sportsmanship

Professionalism is about good sportsmanship and having class. When things don't go perfectly, poise is important. You cannot live as a professional driven by emotions, the words or opinions of others, or by an external system. If you are, then you will struggle to have a long career and may get a reputation as a hothead or worse. If your bus is late, your bib number doesn't have pins, or they run out of water, don't lose your cool.

Whether your experience at a meet is good or bad, always remain respectful of those around you. Be intentional about acknowledging not just the other competitors, but every individual who is at the track that day. People are people, regardless of their position.

Make it a point to find and thank the meet director and meet staff (most of whom are volunteers) for their presence and hard work. Remember that a spot in a meet is not mandatory; there is no requirement that a meet promoter let you compete no matter how good you are. Everyone has bad days and being grateful and respectful might ensure you are invited back even when your performance is less than stellar.

If you stop and consider what goes into putting a meet together, then you should not have a hard time being grateful. You know it can take months of preparation for one meet and without organizers passionate enough to do that, opportunities to compete would be few and far between. How many thank yous do you think the event volunteers get from elite athletes? The small number might shock you. You can bet they do hear all the things that didn't go well. Why not be the person who expresses gratitude for all the unseen work that took place? A small "thank you" can go a long way.

Professionalism is also about how you treat your competitors. Mutual respect is contingent upon how you behave on and off the track. The United States vs. Jamaica sprint rivalry has a lot of history. The rivalry between the two countries is fierce. During the height of my career, I frequently competed against one of the best: Veronica Campbell Brown. Some people don't like this kind of challenge, but the truth is that I was better when I had someone to line up against who challenged me every time I competed. While overall the chatter and fanfare was distracting, Veronica and I never let it consume us. We were cordial, honored the one who was better on that particular day, and respected that we were bringing out the best in each other.

Honoring each other did not mean we were besties hanging out on the weekend, but as true professionals we left it all on the track. There was a point in my career when I began struggling with my weight. I remember Veronica asking me what the problem was, and I said, "I love food." She simply said, "Exercise some discipline and put the fork down!" I felt embarrassment run through me. I could have gotten upset at her, but in processing what she said, I couldn't be angry. This was her way of saying, "You are an outstanding athlete when you are at your best, and I want to compete against you at your best. If food is stopping you from bringing your A game every time we step on the track, then get your eating under control because we have work to do!"

Your event would be far less exciting if you were only competing against yourself. Sometimes you will have the victory and other days you will have to deal with defeat. It is important that you acknowledge those who are pursuing their journey alongside you and appreciate their contribution to yours.

Professionals Manage Their Time Well

Build your own work day, creating stability and a routine that promotes a healthy life. You balanced school and track during college and excelled. Now you can dedicate even more time to your new profession. Unfortunately, some beginning athletes convince themselves there is not enough time to continue to invest in their life beyond competing, but that train of thought is flawed.

Whether you are inclined to spend your spare time working on a hobby, taking classes at a community college, getting an advanced degree, pursuing a flexible internship, or volunteering regularly, you must set aside time to continue to grow off the track. The worst mistake you can make is going home to play video games every day, eating because you have nothing better to do, or sleeping all day. Don't waste precious time; be productive.

Learn how to manage your time. Professionals should not make a habit of being fashionably late. Be on time. *For real.* People notice when you're late to practice, call times for the bus, and events. Not only does this make you look bad, it puts out a vibe that you don't value other people's time. Being late and missing appointments communicates to those around you that you are only worried about yourself. Last minute cancellations because something more fun came up is as unprofessional as it gets. That is time that someone set aside for you and it is time they could have been working for someone else and making money.

For example, if you are lucky enough to be invited, don't commit to attending the USATF athlete retreat or the annual meeting and then decide you would rather stay at home that weekend. This does not feel like it is coming out of your pocket, but it reduces the pool of resources available for everyone. Time is money for all involved.

Professionals Value and Invest In Support

There is a lot of responsibility associated with being a professional. However, with the right attitude and a good group of people to help you, success is achievable. Investing in those who are invested in your success is one of the most important decisions you'll make as a professional. Fair compensation for good work will produce major returns. Start by finding an agent.

CHAPTER 2

AGENTS

"As an agent, my job is to help my clients achieve their dreams. Being an agent is not just about working on contracts or securing meet entries, it's also about helping clients build a long-term plan for their career. As world-class athletes, my clients work extremely hard and the most important thing I can do for them is to make sure they have the support they need to maximize their potential."

-Merhawi Keflezighi, Track and Field Agent

What is an agent or an athlete representative? Simply put, this individual is responsible for negotiating and managing the various aspects of athletes earning a living by participating in the sport. Negotiating on behalf of the athlete for sponsorship, race attendance, and appearance fees are part of their duties. An agent in good standing should have completed the registration process with both the International Association of Athletics Federations (IAAF) and USATF. Their certification requirements include passing an exam, paying a fee, securing liability insurance, having a background check, safe sport training, and annual ongoing education.

When you finish school or decide to leave college early, an agent is generally the first part of that process. You may be wondering, "Where do I find an agent?" If you are an athlete that has the potential of earning a shoe contract, then it is likely the agents will come looking for you. If not, you can go to the USATF website to view a list of agents.

For athletes still in college, this is exciting, but also an area to exercise caution. It is important not to do anything that could jeopardize your eligibility to compete at the NCAA level before you make the decision to give it up voluntarily. Familiarize yourself with the NCAA rules. When you know the rules you will be able to protect yourself from agents who might not be following the rules.

Here is a breakdown of the ways a track and field student-athlete could lose their eligibility to compete by no longer being considered an amateur according to the NCAA rules 12.1.2 Amateur Status (as of January 2019).

12.1.2 Amateur Status. (Revised: 4/25/02 effective 8/1/02, 4/23/03 effective 8/1/03, 4/29/10 effective 8/1/10)

An individual loses amateur status and thus shall not be eligible for intercollegiate competition in a particular sport if the individual:

(a) Uses his or her athletics skill (directly or indirectly) for pay in any form in that sport;

(b) Accepts a promise of pay even if such pay is to be received following completion of intercollegiate athletics participation;

(c) Signs a contract or commitment of any kind to play professional athletics, regardless of its legal enforceability or any consideration received, except as permitted in Bylaw 12.2.5.1;

(d) Receives, directly or indirectly, a salary, reimbursement of expenses or any other form of financial assistance from a professional sports organization based on athletics skill or participation, except as permitted by NCAA rules and regulations;

(e) Competes on any professional athletics team per Bylaw 12.02.12, even if no pay or remuneration for expenses was received, except as permitted in Bylaw 12.2.3.2.1;

(f) After initial full-time collegiate enrollment, enters into a professional draft (see Bylaw 12.2.4); or

(g) Enters into an agreement with an agent.

Here are some additional thoughts about each of those points:

a) Using athletics skill for pay in that sport
- If a student-athlete receives salary or compensation
- If a student-athlete receives educational expenses (from a third party that is not in the form of a scholarship)

b) Accepts promise of pay
- Agreements that are written or verbal for future compensation are the same as contemporaneous contracts

c) Signs a contract to play professional athletics
- If the intent is for the student-athlete to become a professional, this would make them ineligible even if the contract turns out not to be a legal one

d) Receives a salary from a professional sports organization
- If a student-athlete is a member of a club with a professional team and accepts a salary, even without a contract

e) Competes on a pro team with limited exceptions
  • We see this a lot with our international prospective student-athletes (PSAs) where they get "called up" to the pro team level

f) Enters into a pro draft after becoming a student-athlete
  • Not really an issue in track

g) Enters into an agreement with an agent
  • The agreement can be written or verbal
  • The agreement can start immediately or can be for future representation
  • Accepting benefits from an agent can make you ineligible even if you aren't immediately considered a professional

Here are some exceptions:

12.1.2.4.1 Exception for Prize Money Based on Performance -- Sports Other Than Tennis. In sports other than tennis, an individual may accept prize money based on his or her place finish or performance in an athletics event. Such prize money may not exceed actual and necessary expenses and may be provided only by the sponsor of the event. The calculation of actual and necessary expenses shall not include the expenses or fees of anyone other than the individual (e.g., coach's fees or expenses, family member's expenses). (Adopted: 4/25/02 effective 8/1/02, Revised: 12/12/06 applicable to any expenses received by a prospective student-athlete on or after 8/23/06, 4/26/12, 1/19/13 effective 8/1/13, 4/25/18)

12.1.2.4.7 Exception for Training Expenses. An individual (prospective or enrolled student-athlete) may receive actual and necessary expenses [including grants, but not prize money, whereby the recipient has qualified for the grant based on his or her performance in a specific event(s)] to cover development training, coaching, facility usage, equipment, apparel, supplies, comprehensive health insurance, travel, room and board without jeopardizing the individual's eligibility for intercollegiate athletics, provided such expenses are approved and provided directly by the U.S. Olympic Committee (USOC), the appropriate national governing body in the sport (or, for international student-athletes, the equivalent organization of that nation) or a governmental entity.

Help in the Transition

I was lucky to have my coach with me when the time came to decide whether or not to give up my eligibility. She had my best interest in mind and knew all the proper steps to take. The first thing she did was reach out to our athletic department compliance team and asked for their involvement from the beginning. From that point on, they were present at the meetings with agents.

Many will have parents who want to be very involved in this process. While my parents were not part of my process, this is something you may want to consider depending on your relationship with them, their knowledge of the sport, and how much mutual trust you have.

Parents need to know that having a son or daughter who is a world-class athlete does not make them a world-class advisor in regards to track and field or professional sports. Your parents may have good intentions, but they are not experts, so it is important that you find an expert who has experience to mentor you.

A trusted mentor as part of your entourage is a vital piece of the puzzle in the area of support. This is often the person who, in an effort to help, never charges you a penny and is always willing to give you unbiased, valuable advice. Having someone who will research the questions you don't know to ask and be willing to take their time to help you through the process is invaluable. This person is not always your parent, and for most people it should not be. This person will bring you up when you are down, support you through success and failures, and make sure that you remain grounded.

The Value of Agents

Agents usually work for multiple athletes, but they also keep looking for those with talent who may be new clients. Some agents specialize in the same way that we do as athletes, so they may only represent specific event groups. For example, they may only take clients who are in shot-put or who are sprinters. However, in general, agents are looking for athletes who have the most earning potential. They are business people, and the more money the athletes they represent make, the more money they will make.

Being new to this world, you will depend heavily on your agent's experience because it is very valuable. You will learn together, build together, and grow together. They may even help you through hard times or events. Frequently the agent-athlete relationship is similar to a parent-child relationship. However, it is a business relationship that has specific boundaries that need to be set and respected. As much as we like to think we're grown up at twenty-one years old, it just isn't true. Your agent will have experience you simply don't have, but you cannot go completely "hands off" or you could very well end up with a terrible contract you regret having signed.

Agents are a key and necessary part of a successful professional career. A good agent will be worth every dollar paid and then

some. A bad agent could steal your m
a cot the night before a track meet, po
rightfully yours, and worst of all, nego
All these things could diminish your e
havoc on your ability to provide for you

Let's talk more about what to expec
confident in your ability to choose a go

An Agent Will Get You Into Meets

It is the agent's job to reach out to various meet promoters and let them know you are interested in competing. An agent works with you and your coach to create an itinerary that fits best with your training schedule and overall plan.

You and your coach might look at the available meets and list them in order of preference. From here, the agent reaches out to each of those meet directors letting them know you want to compete. Some may be interested and some may not be. Meet promoters are looking for a variety of athletes. They need some high-level headliners that will sell tickets, but they also need to fill the field of competitors. Not being a headliner does not necessarily put you at a disadvantage. If your agent represents a top athlete, they will sometimes get you into a meet as part of a package deal.

Some will be interested, but not willing to commit just yet. The agent will then come back to you and say something similar to, "Meet one said 'yes,' meet two was a definite 'no,' and meet three said they will wait to see how you run at meet one before making a decision." Now you and your coach can have further discussion about alternative plans and share those with your agent.

Advocate

...lete, your focus and priority is on competing and ...ning well. You do not want every little question people ...e for you to come directly to you, especially at a meet. An agent ...andles answering questions about your availability for events and appearances. They also handle communication related to monetary opportunities not directly related to competing.

A track and field agent will negotiate on your behalf for anything that comes to them, but will not typically seek opportunities to promote you. If you want someone to help you with seeking out marketing and media opportunities to expand your brand, you should look into getting a talent/Public Relations (PR) agent. Track and field agents normally do not have this expertise and will most likely not be able to meet this expectation.

The baseline for what you can expect from your agent is for them to organize your race schedule, negotiate your appearance fees for races, negotiate your shoe contract, handle your travel schedule, and manage hotels and flights. Some offer many services in addition to these, but these are the things you should expect as part of your service agreement.

An Agent Helps with Travel

If you have a contract, you may have a travel budget (more about this in the Sponsorships and Contracts chapter). Athletes need to decide if they want to have their agent pay for and find their flights, or if they would prefer to do it themselves. In most cases, agents book everything for you. This is one thing off your plate, but this means you have less control of departure and landing times and what seat you'll be in. A hands-off approach could end up with you having to wake up at 2:00 am to catch an early flight or sitting in the middle seat by the toilet on every trip you take to Europe.

One benefit you may be missing out on if you don't book you own flights are reward points offered for using your credit card. If you want your agent to handle booking the travel but want to capture the rewards, you can provide your agent with your credit card information so you can still earn rewards. My advice is that if you can afford to book flights yourself, do it. But make sure you track both the flights being booked and the expenses that are incurred. In the off-season, you can enjoy the benefits of all the points you earned.

An organized and transparent agent will track monies paid by the meet for travel and accommodations and will be happy to share those numbers with you. They know that your financial stability keeps them financially sound.

Different meets have different budgets, and in some cases meets may offer travel funds only to certain athletes. Others do not offer travel money at all. Getting an American athlete to a race abroad is expensive. Yet, someone has to pay for it. If you are not offered any travel money, it is your responsibility to get yourself to the meet. This is a frequent occurrence for non-sponsored athletes who need to travel internationally.

There are many agents that use their own money to get an athlete to Europe and then deduct the cost of the ticket out of the prize money. This is a noble effort on the agent's part and often goes unrecognized by the athlete. An agent fronting the money for you to have an opportunity is risky. This leads to some agents having to eat the cost of an athlete's travel when an athlete earns little or nothing.

Interviewing and Choosing An Agent

When the time is right according to the NCAA guidelines agents will reach out to you, and you can meet with them. But there is only so much an agent can learn from one or two meetings or phone calls with an athlete. It is important for you to interview the agent to see if they are the right fit, but also to give them a good flavor for who you are.

One area that is often embellished to entice you is possible contract numbers. Beware of intangible promises. When you are being recruited, base salary numbers will be thrown out that might seem random. As you are speaking to various agents, these numbers should be within a reasonable range from each other. If an agent shares a number that greatly differs from the other agents you interviewed, proceed with caution. Pause and dig in. Ask a lot of questions about how they arrived at that number and what could make that number change. I have known athletes who decided to partner with an agent who said they could make far more than any other agent said, only to find out that they were lied to.

Do not just say "Yes" to the first agent who shows interest in representing you. This is where professional responsibility begins. You must take time to interview them. Make sure you ask the simple things that may be implied from the beginning, and remain objective. Simply signing with an agent who says they will get you the most money, will leave you disappointed more often than not.

In your interview, you are not only trying to gather information, but also gauge the agent's honesty and authenticity. An eager agent can be a very charismatic sales person. While a song and dance can be entertaining, it is important that they know how to do their job.

PRO TIP 👍

Questions to ask a potential agent:

Why did you become an agent?

Why do you want to represent me?

What is a desirable outcome for you from our business relationship?

What has been your best experience representing an athlete?

What has been your worst experience with an athlete?

How do you work through conflict?

What can you do to help me extend the life of my career?

Who are some of your retired athletes and how are they doing now?

May I have the contact information for a few of your current and former athletes so I can talk to them?

Will you help me find a financial professional?

I want a long career. What is your philosophy on the number of events I need per season?

An agent should have a basic idea of what you may be able to earn, but at the end of the day an agent does not decide the dollar amount of your contract; the sponsor paying you does. The agent's job is to work as hard as they can to get you the best deal, but your market value at the time you become a professional is based on a very objective set of criteria of what you bring to the table.

Do some homework on the agent before you meet face to face. Speak to other athletes (a list of athletes each agent represents is on the USATF website). Find other athletes happy to talk candidly about their experience with their agent. It can be challenging to find good information otherwise.

Also make sure you understand how payments will work. Most agents will collect payments on your behalf, take their cut, and then pay you. You do have the option of collecting your money and then paying the agent. This keeps the agent more alert and engaged because they want to make sure they get paid. Once again this will require you to be organized financially. Either way there should be a system in place for you to track funds. A google sheet both of you can see is a great idea.

Finally, once you decide on an agent after interviewing several, call the other agents you spoke with to let them know that you have made a decision. This is part of being a professional. You would not want to be left waiting to find out whether or not a potential employer was going to hire you. It would be better just to know you didn't get the job so you can move on. You don't want to burn any bridges. This is also a good time to give them feedback as to why you chose a different agent, if you can do it in a respectful way.

It is wonderful when you choose the right agent from the beginning and can work with one person for the duration of your career, but it doesn't always happen like that. An agent contract is renewable every year, so if you want to move on after a season you are well within you right to do so. Be mindful that while moving on from working with an agent can be done, you are still obligated to continue to compensate them the agreed upon percentage for any contracts they negotiated on your behalf. This may also make you less attractive to another agent because they will only be collecting a percentage of your prize monies.

The contract with your agent begins on the date you sign and, unless renewed, it remains in effect until December 31 of that year. However, in September of the contract year the agent may notify you that the contract will be renewed for the following calendar year unless, on or before December 1, you notify the agent in writing that you have chosen not to renew the contract.

Agent Compensation

Agents are performing a service and are compensated for the service being provided. They need to earn a living, provide for their family, and save for retirement just like you. They are not your personal servants. As you continue to train your mind to operate as a business owner, you need to remember this. Agents are looking for athletes who will help them earn an income.

Typically, an agent earns 15%-20% of the contract and prize money they negotiate on behalf the athlete. While I am not crazy about these percentages knowing that a coach also has to be compensated, it is currently the way the industry is and you have to plan accordingly. If you understand this, you won't be offended or resentful of them for the price they charge. Rather you will see them as a business partner who helps you win so they can also win. Athletes get into financial troubles because they do not take these things into consideration when planning for expenses.

PRO TIP 👍

A good agent has to be great at communication and understanding. You learn that every athlete is different in how they live, prepare, and what they need to perform at their best. An agent will invest time to learn your personality. It can be simple things like whether you want them with you when warming up or not. Some athletes prefer to put headphones on, get in the zone, and do not like to talk at all. Others want their agent there to talk to because it keeps them calm. It's the same post-race. Good days are easy; rough days can be hard. What to say? What not to say? But that's about being perceptive to an individual's personality.

Brad Yewer
Agent, Flynn Sports Management

CHAPTER 3

DEVELOPING, EMERGING, & ELITE ATHLETES

"I worked at least fifty hours a week and sometimes 65 to 75 hours a week while training. I would leave for work at 7:30am, get to work early, open the store, work until 2:00pm, train for two hours and work out, come back around 5:00pm, close the store at 10:00pm, drive home 45 minutes, and repeat."

- Matt Hemmingway, Olympic Silver Medalist, High Jump

If you want to become a professional athlete to get rich and famous or because this is the easiest way for you to earn money, give up now. There is so much more to being a professional athlete. The world has plenty of examples of those with this shallow philosophy who never reach their full potential.

No career or fame will satisfy your need for significance. You need to have your identity and worth sorted out or you will spend your life chasing external things that do not satisfy you and never will. Decide now why you want to become a professional athlete.

In track and field there are various levels of athletes, and since there is no easy or clear definition of these categories, I have taken the liberty of breaking the athletic levels into three groups.

Developing Athletes: Developing athletes are NCAA All-Americans who have completed their NCAA eligibility but are not ranked in the top eight nationally. Maybe they have the standard to compete at nationals, however, they have not been contacted by any agents. Developing athletes want to commit to continuing to compete, but feel they need two or three more years to develop fully. For those in this category, making the choice to pursue track and field needs careful consideration. They will have to balance training with working full time and possibly seek financial support from a family member. Just because they are not being pursued by agents, doesn't mean that they will not develop into a professional athlete.

Emerging Elite Athletes: Emerging elite athletes have the potential to make an international or national team. They may be an NCAA All-American, or may have even won an NCAA championship, but failed to make an international team. This means they have the talent and skills to be a professional, but likely have not yet signed a contract. If they have signed a contract, it is modest. These athletes are usually eligible to be placed into the USA Track and Field Tier System.

Elite Athletes: Elite athletes are those who have earned a place on an international team representing Team USA. While some NCAA athletes may fall into this category, most will not. An NCAA athlete who has not yet completed his/her eligibility but has performed so well either during a college competition or as a member of Team USA that they have the opportunity to leave college early to pursue professional sports fit into this category. This is less than 3% of college athletes.

Over 1 million athletes participate in high school track. A little less than 60,000 go on to compete at the NCAA level. That is 5% that go from high school to college. If we assume that 5% also go pro that would mean 3,000 athletes go pro each year. We know that the USA Championships have between 800-1,100 participants. Of those, many are veteran athletes, so it is safe to say that you need to be outstanding to have a shot.

While I have attempted to create some separation in performance levels, it is important to note that all three categories of this system will have unsponsored athletes. By unsponsored I mean they do not have a stable means of income. This is where you gasp and say, "That's not fair. If I am in the top category surely I am going to be ballin'!" It may not be fair (many things about this sport are not), but you are here by choice and no one is making you choose to be a professional athlete. Earnings will vary by event, performance, marketability, and many other factors. Being elite simply isn't enough.

Real Talk for the Developing Athlete

Elite and emerging elite athletes have some resources available to them. Developing athletes on the other hand are truly like entrepreneurs. They have to pull up their boot straps and do much of the work on their own.

You make a choice to participate in the sport, and it is important to educate yourself about what is available. One of the greatest sources of "income" for many athletes in Track and Field are the grants from the USATF Foundation. To learn about resources talk to other athletes. Get involved. Start by connecting with the AAC (Athletes Advisory Committee) to learn about current events, governance of the sport, and how to contribute to the collective athlete voice. Understanding the inner workings of the sport will diminish the disappointment and allow your voice to be heard.

You may have no idea how you're going to make it work without a contract (or even with a modest one) but many have and are currently doing so. Don't let lack of stable earnings deter you. Own it and be proactive about creating ways to work around it. Some athletes spend way too much time focusing on the lack of resources available to them rather than making the most of what they have, so that someone can see their potential and come alongside to support them.

The cost of simply living is always your responsibility. The cost to train and compete to pursue your passion is also your responsibility.

- How will you pay for rent, food, and care for your body?
- Where will you work out?
- Who will coach you?
- How will you get your passport and the necessary visas for some countries?
- Will you enter yourself into meets?
- Are you going to reach out to meet promoters on your own?

Being able to answer to these questions will require work and research. You have to work for what you want. You can and should be a participant in the process. You may face significant challenges, but the payoff will come later when your performances improve.

The IAAF has all of their meets listed on their website (www.iaaf.org). After you identify meets you'd like to compete in, find the meet director and contact him/her. Let him/her know you are interested in competing. Be respectful and even if you don't get the response you are looking for, keep knocking.

When sending emails and messages, take extra care to ensure there are no typos! Using proper English is incredibly important when it comes to having people take you seriously. Have someone like a family member or friend who is more adept at writing than yourself look over important emails and documents before you send them off. This is more important than you might think!

You may find it helpful to create different templates for communication you do frequently. This can be done easily using the canned response feature in Gmail. For example, say you are reaching out to an event promoter and you have already written up a template email for promoters. Insert the canned response, plug in the specific details and names, and send. This saves so much time! Instead of writing a brand-new email each time, most of what you need to say is already written. In time you'll realize ways to make that email better and you can change the template.

Also, don't underestimate the power of a thank you note. Make them remember you!

Budget to get yourself to Europe. If a meet promoter doesn't have to spend the money, they may be more likely to accept you into the meet. This will cost you at first, but with a few wins under your belt you will no longer be paying for your own travel. It is worth the investment.

Create a spreadsheet that details the when, why, and where of each event. Also, list any relevant contacts, information, or questions that may pertain to each one. This can be done pretty quickly in Google Sheets or Microsoft Excel and will help you keep track of events and what money is coming in and going out. The AAC has a great spreadsheet on their site (usatfaac.org) to help you track income.

Just because you have't gotten a big sponsor yet does not mean you are without options. Be creative. There are millions of people in this world and many are looking for a team to be on. Here are a few ideas to get you started.

> **Start local:** The people of your hometown would probably be thrilled to help you pursue your Olympic dream. Maybe you can convince your local grocery store to sponsor their hometown athlete by offering free groceries. Free is always in the budget!

> **Tell your story:** Creating a brand and building your platform is imperative to attract support. AthleteBiz is a great resource to help you.

> **Volunteer:** Choose with a cause you are passionate about. Then, build a relationship with the members of the organization.

Like any business venture, participating in sports is a risk. Sometimes you win, and sometimes you walk away empty handed, left to figure out how to feed yourself and pay your bills. Let's say you get 6th at the USA indoor championships, and you did not make the international team you were trying out for. However, the staff selects you to take part in a relay, but unfortunately you all get disqualified. You just traveled and competed and didn't earn a dollar, but not only that, you spent money because you had to pay out of pocket to travel and compete in the USATF Championships. Now what? Unfortunately, this is the cost associated with choosing to compete.

You have to believe in your dream more than anyone else and put in the work to get there. If you are not putting in the work, no one else will do it for you. Hard work and grit can many times be more impressive than talent. Keep going!

CHAPTER 4

SPONSORSHIPS & CONTRACTS

"Sponsorships are the cornerstone of the profession of track and field. In order to maximize your sponsorship value, you need to learn the language of the standard contract."

- Adam Nelson, Olympic gold medalist, shot put

I have alluded to sponsorships and contracts or lack thereof in previous chapters. This is how athletes get paid. We are not employees of USA Track and Field. The most stable and sought after way of earning a contract is via a shoe company. Having a shoe company as a sponsor is crucial to your viability as a professional athlete. While there are other sponsorship opportunities, currently shoe companies are the main support system for professional track and field athletes.

There are many things to consider as you are going through the process of committing to a contract. Do not rush! Sometimes companies make it seem urgent that you sign immediately. That is not ideal and is seldom necessary. This contract will determine quite a bit about your financial future over the next few years of your career. While there may be pressure to sign while at a competition, choosing to sign or not to sign may have significant monetary implications.

You don't want to sign in a hurry, then out-perform your contract and be rewarded with a candy bar. What I mean by that is the company may have a bonus in place for if you beat a certain time or distance, but after you reach that and perform even better, they may not have additional bonuses in place. So you'll want to look at that carefully and suggest adding bonuses with even better times or distances in the contract. When you perform well, everyone wins and a sponsor should be happy to compensate you for that.

Hopefully, contract negotiations start with numbers within the ballpark of what you were told by the agent when you interviewed them. If not, pause and ask what caused the difference in the estimate provided and what is currently being offered. This may be a sign your agent "sold you to sell you" and should be considered a red flag in building a trusting relationship.

However, there are some factors that can cause a large change in numbers, your performance being one of them and timing another. Did everyone else sign ahead of you and now there is little left in your potential sponsor's signing budget for the remainder of the year? Is a company setting aside major funds for a big fish they are in negotiations with? This is hard to know, but it is still something to consider.

Let's proceed assuming that all is right with the world and you have two deals on the table within a reasonable range of one another. One is $100,000 and the other is $110,000. At first glance you may say, "This is a no brainer. An extra $10,000 means this company values me more." This is why paying attention to the fine print and details is essential. The $110,000 contract may say, "*If you're not one of the top three in the world, your compensation will be reduced 20%.*"

The $100,000 contract may say, *"If you're not top ten in the world, your compensation will be reduced 20%."* Now this requires some thought. While we all think we are superman/woman, one injury can cause you to miss meets and affect your world ranking. Dropping to $88,000 for not being in the top three or dropping to $80,000 for not being in the top ten is a huge difference in finances.

While your agent should point out subtle differences such as these and help you choose the contract that is clearly better for you, you need to read the entire contract yourself! You don't want to be caught off guard by things that were not obvious initially. Focus on the fine print.

PARTS OF A CONTRACT

Base Salary: A base salary is the amount you can count on for the year. You will get a certain amount per year which can go up or down from one year to the next. The wonderful part about a base salary is the consistency it creates in organizing your finances, at least on an annual basis. Most shoe companies pay quarterly, which means you will receive payment four times a year. Big sums feel amazing when you receive them, but it is important that you plan to make those funds last three months. Also, don't forget your agent and your taxes have to be paid from each check as well. It is important to note that your base salary could be $0 which would mean you have a bonuses only contract.

Bonuses: Bonus structures are created based on how well your sponsor thinks you can perform. You earn rewards for good performances. Criteria for performance bonuses can be general, such as a time or distance at any meet, or more specific like first place at a Diamond League meet.

For example, if you are a long jumper who is currently jumping 6.90 they may start provide a bonus amount at 7.17, 7.25, and 7.30. Usually you do not get a bonus for achieving all three, but the amount associated with your best performance.

Anything is possible, which is why you should clarify your bonus structure by asking lots of questions. Achieving records can lead to much larger pay days. Meet records, American records, and world records might get you a bonus and possibly a rollover to increase your salary going forward.

Rollovers: Essentially, a rollover will add to your base salary in the following year. If you win Olympic gold, you might get a $100,000 salary increase for all years remaining in your contract. If you win silver you may get a $50,000 salary increase, and if you win bronze you may get a $30,000 salary increase. A rollover is usually only a consideration when there is a medal or record involved.

Length: One of the other things to remember about a contract is that it is an agreement for a specified amount of time. Contract lengths vary widely. Most frequently you see a four-year contract or a four-year contract with a fifth-year option. At some point your contract will end, so if you are not ready to stop competing, prepare yourself for the negotiation of another deal.

It is hard to foresee what will happen over the length of a contract. You may be on top of the world when the contract is being written and injured when it is time to negotiate. Each contract negotiation starts with a clean slate and is not based on what you have accomplished, but what sponsors feel you can accomplish going forward. Having five medals may be worth something to you, but a company is not compensating you on your past performance. They are banking on your continued success and future performance.

Education: If you are being lured out of school early, make sure your sponsor is willing to pay for the remainder of your education. Your degree is valuable and you don't want to have to pay out of pocket for something that you were already receiving for free. Some universities are beginning to allow student-athletes to complete their degree even after choosing to give up their eligibility because it helps their graduation rates. If your school is not willing to pay, your sponsor should be.

Having your sponsor pay provides flexibility in the event it is more convenient to complete your education at a different university. If a company finds you valuable enough to sign you without your eligibility being complete, then they will likely think your education is a worthwhile investment.

Coaching: If you are signing a contract for a large sum of money, then you can bet the sponsor is going to want to have some say in how to make the most of their investment. It is quite possible that they will be directing you to a coach of their choice. Wait... what?! Yes, signing with a particular shoe company may also affect the coaching choices that are available to you.

Some professional coaches are employed by specific brands and can only work with athletes that are sponsored by that brand. You don't want to be a world-class hurdler that is unable to find a coach because of limitations like these, so do that research before you sign on the dotted line. You may be saying, "Well, I will just stay with my college coach then." Unfortunately, some sponsors don't want you to train with a school that is in conflict with their brand.

Coaching Stipend: A coaching stipend is an allocation of dollars for you to pay your coaches. You need a coach, and they need an income. It is a necessary expense that can either come out of your pocket or your sponsor's. Don't be bashful in asking them to help with this. You may get some discretion over how it is paid and to whom. For, example you may be able to say you are your own coach and pay yourself some extra. (This is not ideal unless you are actually coaching yourself. Don't be stingy.) Another possibility is splitting the coaching stipend up and paying various people on your team such as your weight and event coaches. However, the sponsor may be very specific about how they will allow you to use these funds.

Travel Allocation: Travel allocation is money allocated to travel expenses. These funds can help defray the costs associated with traveling to compete, seeing a medical person, or having performance testing done. When you get invited to a meet, usually there is a flat travel amount provided, but your ticket may cost more than that. You will need to make up the difference, and this travel allocation will help.

Other ways to use this money might include paying for a single room at a meet only covers the cost if you share a room with another athlete. Another example is upgrading to extra legroom on long flights so you can recover faster and compete better after travel. This can also cover baggage fees, especially if you do a field event and have to travel with your equipment. In addition, it can cover other miscellaneous travel expenses like airport parking, food, gas money, etc. These expenses are often paid for up front by either the athlete or the coach and then reimbursed by the company later.

Medical Allocation: Your health and well-being are to your profession what a working calculator is to an accountant. It needs to stay in excellent working order.

Medical allocation can be used for massages, acupuncture, nutritionist visits, routine maintenance at a chiropractor, or traveling to see a specialist after an injury. There are some well-known physiotherapists in Europe and Canada that require you travel to them and compensate them for their expertise. You also have to pay for your food and housing while you are there. These costs can add up quickly.

Your body is your business. Prioritizing maintenance to keep it healthy is imperative. These expenses are often paid for up front by either the athlete or the coach and then reimbursed by your sponsor later.

Apparel/Shoes/Gear: Some contracts will include an account for you to purchase things online and an allowance to buy training, competition, and leisure clothing and equipment. This stuff feels free but it is important to remember that it is taxable and at the end of the year you will see a 1099 for this. This is why a good accountant is important (more about accountants later).

Appearances: Sponsors want to leverage their ambassadors on and off the track. This benefits both you and them. However, you want your contract to specify how many off-track appearances you have to attend. Otherwise, you may find yourself bombarded with obligations. They may want to showcase you at an event such as a fundraiser or gala, shoot an ad campaign for the launch of a new product, or have you come to their headquarters to speak to their employees. This is essential to a lucrative business relationship. If you want to be showcased in promotions, this is a good time to say so.

On the flip side, many times athletes are disappointed to see models or other athletes used in their sponsor's promotions and wonder why they weren't invited to be part of them. However, there is no requirement for your sponsor to do so, and it is important to manage your expectations from the beginning so you don't feel let down if it does not happen.

Meet Requirements: In addition to sponsoring athletes individually, shoe companies also sponsor track meets. If they are sponsoring a meet, you can bet they are going to want to showcase their athletes there. Making your attendance at a particular meet mandatory will affect the way you plan your schedule. Check to see if there are particular meets your sponsor expects expect you to compete in every year and what the consequences or make up opportunities are should you have to miss one of those meets due to injury or other emergency.

Additionally, you will be required to compete in a minimum number of meets each year. This assures you don't collect the paycheck without ever competing. Ask yourself whether the number of meets they are requiring is fair as a minimum.

Under what circumstances would you not be able to meet this requirement? One situation that young ladies frequently fail to consider is pregnancy. What happens if you get pregnant you don't compete for a season? Depending on the language of your contract, you could be cut completely. You may say to your sponsor, "You can't discriminate against me because I am pregnant!" Your sponsor will say, "This has nothing to do with your pregnancy. You didn't compete, plain and simple!" This is why it is important to pay attention to the details of the contract.

Keep a copy of your contract on file at home and make sure you remind yourself of the finer details regularly. Don't have an "out of sight, out of mind" mentality with your sponsorship contracts.

The Official Sponsor of USATF: Corporations want as much publicity and exposure as possible, so they pay money to athletes to represent them. These sponsors want to see their logo in every place possible. The more visible the athlete, the better sponsorship opportunities available. As an athlete, you may choose to enter into a sponsorship contract with one of the various shoe companies.

Ultimately the goal of any track and field athlete is to compete as a member of Team USA and line up against other countries to show athat you are, in fact, the best in the world. If you earn this privilege, you will wear official team gear and that gear will be Nike. Nike is the sponsor of USA Track and Field, and every American athlete who competes as an official team member on an international team is required to wear Nike regardless of who their actual individual sponsor may be. While this has been great for USATF, as they now have more resources to work with (and some of those resources directly benefit athletes), it diminishes some of the marketability for those athletes whose personal sponsor is a shoe company other than Nike.

For example, if you decided to sign a contract with Adidas as your personal sponsor, you will be wearing their clothing as you compete throughout the season and they will compensate you for that. For a company like Adidas, how do you think they feel when you are wearing Nike on the largest platform with the most exposure? While it hasn't caused other brands to remove themselves from the picture completely, it has impacted the nature of contracts and availability of offers from companies where there is a potential for the athlete to make Team USA.

Other Ways to Make Money

Not everyone will have a contract, but you can still make a living without one. You don't have to get major sponsorships right out of the gate. Don't underestimate the possibility of gaining sponsorship elsewhere just because a shoe contract is not an option for you right now. As a businessperson you will need to be creative with different ways you could be compensated. Start with your hometown, local grocery store, or bank. Every corporation wants to support their hometown hero. The following sections list other options for earning, but don't feel limited by these options.

Prize Money: Prize money is simple. You get money based on the place you finish in a particular track meet. Some meets will have higher prize money than others. Some will pay all eight places and others will only pay the top three finishers. Every event will pay different amounts and there is really no standard. It has become harder to make a living only from prize money as there are less meets now than in the past, but it is still possible.

Do your research to find the latest U.S. meets by going to the USA Track and Field website and the International Circuit by going to the IAAF website. Here are some of the prize money charts and explanations for bigger events.

Olympic Games: $0.00. Just to be clear, you don't get prize money at the Olympic Games. At the time this book was written (2019), USATF will provide $25,000 for gold, $15,000 for silver, and $10,000 for bronze. USOC provides $37,000 for gold, $22,500 for silver, and $15,000 for bronze.

While $62,000 is a reasonable salary in America, it is probably not in line with what you were expecting as an Olympic gold medalist.

OLYMPIC GAMES

	INDIVIDUAL	RELAYS
Gold	$25,000	$37,000
Silver	$15,000	$22,500
Bronze	$10,000	$15,000

PRIZE MONEY (USD)

Sponsors will direct your earning potential beyond the funds above. This will be impacted by your story and your brand. The long-term benefits from standing on the podium can bring extraordinary financial gain; however, these benefits will not automatically come because you performed well.

IAAF World Championships: Yes, it is true you could get more money from getting a medal at the IAAF World Championships than you could earn from winning an Olympic medal. While it is safe to assume some sponsorship opportunity will come from being a medalist, if you didn't have a sponsor heading into the World Championships there are no guarantees. Once again, this may not be fair, but it is important to be aware of this reality.

IAAF WORLD CHAMPIONSHIPS

	INDIVIDUAL	RELAYS
Gold	$60,000	$80,000
Silver	$30,000	$40,000
Bronze	$20,000	$20,000
4th	$15,000	$16,000
5th	$10,000	$12,000
6th	$6,000	$8,000
7th	$5,000	$6,000
8th	$4,000	$4,000

PRIZE MONEY (USD)

IAAF Diamond League: The IAAF Diamond League encompasses 32 Diamond Disciplines, following a championship style model. Athletes earn points at the qualification meetings to qualify for the final of their discipline. Each of the disciplines is staged six or four times before the final. At each of the 12 qualification meetings, athletes are awarded 8, 7, 6, 5, 4, 3, 2 or 1 points for ranking

1st to 8th respectively. The top 8 (100m, 100/110m hurdles and technical events except HJ/PV) or top 12 athletes (middle/long distance and HJ/PV) will be awarded a start at the final. In the 200m, 400m and 400m hurdles, the top 7 athletes qualify for the final. In case of a tie, the best legal performance of the qualification phase wins.

IAAF DIAMOND LEAGUE

	QUALIFY x12 POSSIBLE	FINALS $ INCREASE
1st	$10,000	$50,000
2nd	$6,000	$20,000
3rd	$4,000	$10,000
4th	$3,000	$6,000
5th	$2,500	$5,000
6th	$2,000	$4,000
7th	$1,500	$3,500
8th	$1,000	$2,000

PRIZE MONEY (USD)

The winner at the final of each Diamond Discipline will become "IAAF Diamond League Champion" and be awarded a Diamond Trophy, $50,000 prize money, and a wild card for the IAAF World Championships (certain conditions apply).

Appearance Fees: The appearance fees are as the name implies. You appear and you get paid. All you have to do is participate in the competition. Meet promoters want to sell tickets. To do so they have to put together an amazing event. If you are a reigning gold medalist, you carry enough influence to put butts in the seats. Everyone wants to see a star!

To ensure the best athletes are present and incentivized to perform, the meet promoters are willing to guarantee a sum. The amount is negotiated between your agent and the meet promoter. Keep in mind that the appearance fee is not only based on your past performance, but also on relationship. If your agent is a jerk or inexperienced it could cost you. If you are unprofessional or hard to work with, it can affect the amount you are paid.

The other thing is that you have to take your agent's word on what the appearance fee is. Seldom is there a written document provided to let you know what the agreement is. Politics matter as much in track and field as any other career, sometimes more. It is difficult to know what a standard appearance fee is and whether or not you are getting a fair amount. It would be nice if there was more transparency in the process, but unfortunately it is subjective. There have been many stories of athletes defeating certain competitors numerous times, and the competitor receiving a better appearance fee. It is all relative to negotiation. If you are unhappy with the work your agent is doing, refer back to the previous chapter to understand your rights when terminating an agreement.

There are many ways to be compensated for participating in this sport. Research available opportunities, read the fine print, and know your options.

CHAPTER 5

SELECTING YOUR TRACK FAMILY

"When coaching a post collegiate athlete, it's important for the coach to help the athlete grow through not only the seasons of a budding athlete, but also guide them as they transition to life after college. No matter how big they get as a professional/Olympian/etc., there are always teaching moments when we as coaches need to be there to help guide the athlete."

-Amy Deem, Head Coach University of Miami, & Track and Field Team Head Coach 2012 Women's Olympic Team

We started this book with the process of choosing an agent, but we all know that an athlete without a coach is like peanut butter without jelly. A great coach will take an athlete far beyond their raw talent. You might know a lot about your event, which is why you became a professional, but don't be arrogant and think you don't need a coach. You do, and you need a good one.

The skills required to be a good coach are technical, personal, and professional. A good coach knows as much about communication and emotional intelligence as they do about the technique and mechanics of your specific event.

Let's walk through what finding the right coach could look like.

Should I Stay With My College Coach?

Let's say you have developed a bond with your college coach and have experienced much success under their direction. It would be nice to be coached by them, but it may not be a possibility. Some college coaches are allowed to coach professional athletes while others are strictly prohibited from doing so. Even if allowed, some coaches choose not to coach any elites because it will require extra time and effort that would diminish their focus from coaching their college athletes.

College coaches will prioritize their time based on their obligation to the university that employs them. If you choose to work with a college coach, you have to realize their time will be divided. As an elite athlete ask yourself, are you okay not being the center of attention?

NCAA rules limit the amount of time you can spend training with NCAA athletes when you become a professional. If you stay with your college coach you could lose your training partners. If you are the sole elite athlete training at your university, you may frequently find yourself training alone. Ask yourself if you'll be okay with your training environment looking different than it did in college.

Considering a New Coach

Finding a new coach is much like starting to date. You are trying to understand whether they are trustworthy and a good match for you, but you won't really know until you have committed to being in the relationship. Track is a mostly individual sport, and everyone has a unique skill set and personality. You want a coach that can tune into your special needs and coach you as an athlete, not just coach your event. A good coach seeks the development of both the person and the athlete.

The track and field community is really small; everybody knows everybody. Talk to other athletes who have worked with a certain coach, and look at the accomplishments of athletes they have coached. You shouldn't base your decision solely on what someone else says, but getting various opinions helps. There will probably be a number of people who have worked with the potential coach in some capacity. Be ready with good questions that will tell you whether they have the characteristics you are looking for. Listen for other positive and negative points, but realize ultimately you are trying to decide whether they will be a good fit for you.

Some questions to ask and things to consider are:

- "What do you think of my long-term potential?" This will help you understand more about whether the coach has your longevity in mind.
- "Tell me about your coaching style. Do you prefer to yell or offer rewards or words of praise?" Compare their coaching style to what motivates you.
- "Are you affiliated with a certain shoe company?" Some coaches can only coach athletes who are sponsored by their employer. Remember this when you are negotiating your shoe contract.
- "Do you have official training times? Is morning practice mandatory?"
- "Do you have any rules about how or when your athletes will train based on the weather? For example, if it is above 52 degrees will you practice outside? If it is raining, will you reschedule practice for later in the day or will you stay and wait it out until you can practice?"

- "Pertaining to nutrition and supplements, how much guidance do you provide? Is it mandatory to take particular supplements?" A difference in philosophy in this category could be a huge problem.
- Ask yourself, "Are they easy to talk to?"
- Ask yourself, "Do they seem to care about me as a person and not just as an athlete?"

Track is mostly an individual sport, and everyone has a unique skill set and personality. You want a coach that can tune in to your special needs and coach you as an athlete, not just your event. A good coach is about the development of both the person and the athlete.

A good coach will be sharing their understanding of the many topics covered in this book. They will invest time into your well-being in general, making sure you have balance in your life and that you continue developing life skills. They will speak to you in ways that motivate you, and will not discourage you. They will also encourage you to keep things in perspective and to not lose heart if you have a setback.

Compensating Your Coach

It takes years of training and experience to develop expertise in any area. Good coaching is valuable, so your coach needs to be paid. When you're in college, the institution pays the coach. Now that you're a professional, you do. Your coach is providing a service, and as a business owner you need this service to run your business. Everyone needs to earn an income to support themselves, including coaches. If your earnings are low or non-existent, be aware that you are asking the coach to donate their time. Not every coach can do this, and you cannot be angry at them if they cannot coach you for free.

If you can't afford to pay a coach, and they decide to work with you anyway, be grateful! Be respectful of their time. And when you do begin to earn, prioritize having a conversation about compensating them. That is what a professional would do. Your coach shouldn't have to ask you if you are in a position to pay them once you start having success and earning more. They don't have a way of knowing what you are earning other than published prize money from races. When you make money, your team should make money.

There is not a standard structure for how coaches are compensated like there is with agents. At the time of writing of this book, the coaches are in the midst of organizing themselves to create a uniform way of charging, but the agents have been organized for quite a while. Also, athletes are not crazy about the idea of having to give up an additional 15-20% of their earnings to compensate the coach. Because of this, the coaches are entering into this space without much bargaining power and are looking to outside sources to fund their compensation.

For now, coaches create their own structures for how to charge, which varies quite a bit from one to another. Some take a percentage of your race money or contract. Others charge a flat fee (like $1,000 per month for every person who trains with them) or charge a flat annual rate (like $30,000 with half paid up front). Others will just take what is allocated from the coaching stipend provided in your contract. The scenario will be different with every coach and the goal is to find a win-win for both of you.

PRO TIP 👍

The beauty of long distance running is that one's success is a result of the collective efforts of teammates, coaches, and even physics. To be successful, you have to have a great team of goal-driven individuals behind you.

Bernard Lagat
Olympic bronze and silver medalist, 1500m

Training Groups

Now that you have nailed down all the things you should be looking for in a coach, you must broaden the landscape and think about the environment. You need to consider who else will be training with this coach and how this might affect you. Those you will be sharing your training environment with must also be a good fit. You may be thinking, "Who cares about training partners? I can train alone." Few athletes actually train alone and thrive. If you have never trained alone, don't assume you will be just fine without a training group. Accountability is key.

Though track is not a team sport, it is not one where you should expect one-on-one coaching. Track is a small sport with a limited number of coaching options. Most would say that a group is an important part of pushing yourself to the next level, and I tend to agree with this philosophy. It works well to have someone to measure yourself against and push you. When you train alone you may be prone to rationalize missing a day at the track or weight room. Groups can motivate you if you're not on par one day and need the support. However, there are some things you must consider.

The energy of the other people in the training group is important. I encourage you to learn as much as you can about the dynamic of the group before agreeing to join and relocate.

Training groups can be extremely competitive. Healthy competition is good, but beware of athletes who spend their time creating unnecessary drama. Maybe they won't want to train with you, or maybe they are attention hogs and will try to divert the coach's attention to themselves. Will you be okay if you're not getting the same attention as other athletes?

You could be entirely happy with your training group and then one day your arch nemesis shows up and wants to join the group. In reality, you don't have a say in who your coach decides to take on. By denying an athlete access to the group you may be impacting your coach's ability to earn a living.

While picking a coach and a training group go hand in hand, there are some other considerations.

Location, Location, Location

How easy is it to fly in and out of the city where this coach trains? If you are on a budget in a remote location that always requires you to connect just to get to an airport big enough to take you where you are going, this could inflate travel costs quickly. If you won't be near a major airport, ask how long it takes to drive to the nearest major airport or reasonably priced transportation services to get you there.

What is the weather like? Do you train better in the hot or cold? If it is a cold place, is there an indoor training facility? Workouts can't stop because it is snowing. If you have to train inside until April, will that affect your ability to be ready for outdoor season? Most elite camps are based in Florida, California, and Texas because the weather is more conducive. Large distance running groups are based in colder climates. What environment is going to give you the best chance at success?

Consider the cost of living in the city you might relocate to and compare it to where you are currently living. Major cities such as New York or Los Angeles are very expensive to live in without a steady stream of income. Look at the cost of renting a decent apartment or house. Will living there be doable if you are living alone?

Roommates

Living with other athletes is a viable option with pros and cons. It can save you money and motivate you, but the noise and needs of others can also to be a distraction. Do your research and do your best to find out whether you are all going to be a good fit together. What are the criteria for a good fit besides being a focused athlete? You don't run, jump, or throw at home; you carry on with other elements of your life. It would behoove you to find out whether or not the other person/people are clean or messy, night owls or early birds, diet conscious or not, introverts or extroverts.

If you feel like the roommate situations that are available won't be the best fit for you, see if you can afford a studio apartment. Or if living on your own is unaffordable, see if you can rent a room in a house with a family or if there is a mother-in-law suite available with your own bathroom and a kitchenette, which would allow you privacy and reduced rent. Being budget conscious towards expenses and saving as much of your income as possible is key for professional athletes, which we will look at more in detail next.

CHAPTER 6

A FINANCIAL GAME PLAN
EARN, SAVE, SPEND

"Your self-worth and your net worth are not related! You may feel your value is higher than what you are being paid. You are right because you don't have to have money to have value; you have to have values to have value. You can show your self-worth by being responsible with what you have been given."

-Lauryn Williams CFP®

Author's Note: This chapter is essential! You may choose to skim through the other chapters, but stop and spend some time here. Read every word. I am going to tell you the good news about organized finances, and I will cover as much as possible. After you read this chapter, saying, "I didn't know the basics of how to manage my money" will not be an option for you any longer.

You are competing to earn a living. The money you earn during your career can set you up with a strong foundation for the rest of your life. In the words of Benjamin Franklin, "If you fail to plan, you are planning to fail."

Not optimizing their finances is the area many athletes have regrets about at the end of their time competing. They wish they would have started planning sooner, and they wish they would have saved more. They wish they would have found someone to help them. If they did work with someone, they wish they would have asked more questions before engaging that financial advisor who hardly ever gave them any financial advice.

I have seen too many Olympic medalists who have had awesome careers struggling to make ends meet just a year or two after finishing competing. Life after sports is hard enough without having to deal with the realization of knowing you should be a in a different financial position (all the while trying to look as if everything is okay to everyone around you).

Some athletes are fortunate enough to still have a great earning potential after sports. If they didn't maximize planning while competing, they realize they have a second chance and they rebound as a more responsible individual after a rude awakening about how important it is to live below your means and plan ahead. Others spend irresponsibly, don't plan for the future, and have very few skills or abilities that would allow them to earn at the level they did while competing.

I was not foolish with my money, but I could have had a lot more at the end of my career with better guidance. I made many mistakes both on my own and while under the guidance of a financial professional. The two financial advisors I worked with were less than stellar, but I still ended up in a financially sound position. I understood the value of getting help with things I didn't know a lot about and still believe working with a professional is valuable.

My undergraduate degree is in finance and I earned an MBA as well. While I learned a lot in school from both degrees, neither focused on organizing my personal finances. Finally, I found the

CERTIFIED FINANCIAL PLANNER™ certification that is specific to being able to help people navigate all aspects of their financial life. I knew that this would help me and also allow me to help other athletes and young people who want to do the right things with their money, but just don't know where to start.

The transition from sports to life after sports is a hard one. Don't let poor financial planning add more stress to the transition. Good habits now will go a long way for you in the future.

Whatever you are earning, live as if you are earning half that amount. Save the rest! Whether you earn a lot or a little, the key principles to financial stability are the same. Spend less than you earn. Be responsible with what you have. Later is not your friend (in regards to saving). Now is your best friend.

One of the biggest financial mistakes is not mastering the basics before moving on to other financial goals. These basics include having an emergency fund, creating a budget, setting savings goals, and understanding debt and credit. Beyond the basics we will address taxes, retirement and investing, and protecting yourself and others through insurance. Mastering the basics plays an important role in your financial life.

Emergency Fund

Your emergency fund is your true best friend. This is your first area of focus when building wealth. Do not skip this step. The list of events emergency savings might be used for is endless.

What if it doesn't work out with your coach and you have to pick up and leave mid-season? There is a cost to breaking your housing lease and hiring movers, as well as putting a security deposit on your new place. Injury is another good example. If you get hurt in April and it ends your season, you are going to be in a tough spot. If you are not sponsored and depend on prize money as your main source of income, this emergency fund will kick in immediately. If you have a sponsor, you still have your contract, but what if it gets reduced as a result of this injury? What about the extra cost of rehab and physical therapy? You will need this money to meet basic expenses in the coming months and for the expenses related to getting healthy again.

How much do you need? This will vary based on income and basic cost of living, but a good rule of thumb to start with is a minimum of three months of income. If you get paid quarterly, it is easy to calculate that it is one full paycheck you should have set aside. Ultimately, you should try to save six months of income to make sure you are covered. A lot of people get worked up because it seems like a lot of cash on hand, but the security it creates in case of an emergency is priceless.

Saving

Spending less than you earn is a no brainer rule if you want to achieve wealth. Putting a process in place to follow this rule is not always intuitive. Two simple steps will help you achieve this: automate your savings and pay yourself first.

Automation is setting up automatic transfers to move money to your savings account so it is out of sight and out of mind. Paying yourself first is taken care of if you set up automation to happen every time money comes in. Even if you don't choose automation, the pay yourself first mindset says, "I am going to take some of what I just got and put it aside for me."

Those with paycheck-to-paycheck mentality get paid and immediately think, "What bills do I have to cover?" They cover what they can, spend some, then save whatever is left. There is seldom anything left.

A good place to start is saving 10% of your income with a goal of getting to 20%. If you are unsponsored, start with 10% and increase as you can. There is no hard and fast formula, but if you earn $75,000 you should be comfortable saving 15%, and if you earn $100,000 then 20% is doable.

Create a Spending Plan or Plan to Spend

If you don't tell your money where to go then you'll always be wondering where it went. Not knowing the purpose and destination of each dollar you have is the easiest way to waste money and end up in trouble. Tracking can be tedious but being broke is more stressful! You can use old school pen and paper, download a spreadsheet from the internet, or use an app, but planning ahead by allocating every dollar you earn is important.

Debt and Credit

There are lots of myths out there about debt. Some believe there is good debt and bad debt. The concept of good debt is that you are somehow investing in yourself and you may reap the benefit of borrowing now to have a better life in the future. Homes and student loans are examples of these. Bad debt is purchasing things you cannot afford right now and that quickly lose their value. Buying the newest model of a car (when you have one that runs just fine) and making purchases on a credit card you are unable to pay in full each month are examples of bad debt. Ultimately debt is you saying, "I cannot afford this thing right now so I am willing to pay more than it costs (with interest) to have it."

Your credit score judges your ability to take on debt and pay it back, but it doesn't measure your actual financial health. Think of your credit score as your letter grade on your credit report card, which is called the credit report. Your credit score will not affect your day-to-day finances, but it will affect your ability to procure loans for large purchases, like houses. Sometimes large purchases will require you to take on debt, but the overarching financial principal to live by is to avoid debt.

The credit report contains the details of your debt. A good financial habit is to check your credit report every four months. This is to make sure that no fraudulent activity has happened and that the places you do have debt are recording your payments properly. You can check your credit report by going to *www.annualcreditreport.com* and downloading one of the three reports available.

Avoiding Lifestyle Creep

When you go from being a poor college student barely making ends meet to a professional athlete, there are major changes in your resources. People who are not good with money would say, "I earned it so I get to celebrate by spending it." Unfortunately, that temporary joy has major long-term consequences. When you make more, take the opportunity to save more. It is ideal to try keep your spending the same, but if you need to give your lifestyle a raise, do no more than 50 percent. The other 50 percent increase should be going towards your savings.

When I work with athletes who have a sponsor, we create a plan to live off of their most dependable income, which is the contract. We use prize money for various savings goals. When you live as if prize money is extra, you increase your savings rate dramatically and give yourself a lot of wiggle room in getting ahead for life after sports.

Bill Pay

Another popular service offered by some wealth management firms is a bill pay service for pro athletes. They encourage athletes to act entitled, as if we need a "concierge service" to handle our bills. While it feels cool to say, "My people handle that," it further disconnects you from your money. Yes, you are busy. Yes, you travel all over the world. But to believe you don't have time to pay your bills like everyone else is untrue, and finding someone to enable you in this manner can be crippling. You can automate your bills and set reminders for yourself to pay those that can't be automated, all for free. Choosing to have someone provide a bill pay service can be a pretty pricey convenience.

Homebuyer Beware

Buying a home is another area where making the wrong decision can be extremely costly. Some of the popular perceptions are that buying a home is an investment, it is the American dream, it is a tax deduction, and it is the way you show you are financially stable and officially an adult.

Buying a home is a personal decision and should not be based on what society says you should do. For a young athlete this is a particularly risky undertaking. What you qualify for and what you can actually afford are two different things. You may look at the possible monthly mortgage payment and think you can afford it. But are you going to be able to pay the same mortgage payment for the next thirty years? What job is going to allow you enough income to pay the mortgage after you are done competing?

What if you purchase a home and then two years later decide to change coaches? You would be faced with selling, which will probably be at a loss. (There goes your "investment.") Your other options are renting it out or paying a mortgage on an empty house. If you decide to rent out the house, you will end up being a landlord from afar, which means you can either hire a property manager or manage broken appliances and late rent payments on your own.

Buying a home can be a happy and fulfilling event. Just make sure it is right for you.

Investments/Retirement

Once you have a solid foundation in a good budget, emergency fund, and tax plan then you can start to think about investing. My investment philosophy is simple: SAVE, GROW, SAVE, GROW. Use the investment market to grow what you are saving. Many think there is a strategy in which the market will take whatever amount they have, earn large returns, and turn them into overnight millionaires. It is important to focus less on beating the market and more on saving and using the market like a moving walkway to help you get where you want to go. Having enough set aside to grow so that your money can work for you is a key to financial health in your future.

Investments are the main thing many think of when it comes to having organized finances.

Some avoid the market because they don't understand it and don't feel like they have any control over it. Others have heard the stories of terrible advisors and decide to avoid working with someone because they feel they will figure it out on their own eventually. A common pitfall is investing in projects without knowing much about the investment from a business perspective. For example, we know that people need their car washed and hair cut so we think surely car washes and barber shops are good investments. Everyone talks about real estate investing and flipping and it is easy to see that people need places to live and renters need to pay the owner to live in them. These business and real estate investments are alternative investments that are very risky and may tie your money up for a long time.

The stock market has been around for longer than you have been alive. Yes, it has had its ups and downs, but if you ride the wave, history indicates you will likely end up on the upside. I believe you should maximize your traditional investment options before considering investing in alternative investments.

Athletes retire twice: once from sports and then again at the point they never plan to work again. Because we are independent contractors, there is no one setting money aside for our future. If we don't take initiative, we will one day stop working but won't have anything set aside to support ourselves. The following are some traditional ways to invest your savings.

> **Brokerage account:** This is a taxable investment account that can be used at any time. Generally, this is used when you want to set aside funds for a goal that is at least 5 years away. It is better than a savings account because you have the ability to grow your money at a higher rate. You can manage your investments on your own or enlist the help of a financial planner to do it for you. It's a great place to set money aside to be used after sports.

SEP IRA: Until recently this has been the most popular option for those with good income looking to save on taxes and put money away for retirement. It is easy to set up on your own but you need an accountant to help you calculate the amount you can put into your SEP each year. I won't bog you down with the calculation, but it is generally up to 25% of your income and you can put up to $54,000 into it a year. This is meant for long-term retirement and taking money from it prior to retirement will have tax implications and penalties.

Annuities are frequently used inappropriately and something I advise clients to proceed with great caution and ask lots of questions about before making any final decisions. As a young professional you are in the accumulation phase of life, and you need your money to be growing. Your growth potential is limited with an annuity. It is inappropriate for your advisor to place an annuity in your SEP IRA or other retirement account. An annuity provides a tax shelter in an account that already has a full tax shelter. If an annuity is in your SEP IRA or other retirement account you will be paying additional costs for a redundant strategy, and the fees and commission for these products are significant and deliberately mysterious. I would beware of this strategy and the intentions of the person recommending it.

Solo 401(k): This is similar to the 401(k) offered at many places of employment except this is for one person. The thing that makes this more appealing than a SEP-IRA for a serious saver is your ability to put more money away. This too allows you to put a maximum $54,000 away, but the ability to do so comes with a different set of rules. You are the employer and the employee so you get to make a contribution as each. Setup for this is a bit more tedious but could be worth it in the right scenario.

Traditional IRA: You can put $6,000 into this account each year. In creating a mindset about how much is appropriate to save, this should be your baseline. Try to save at least $6,000 every year, no matter what level earnings you have. The government rewards you for saving for your future by providing some tax savings for your contributions. You will pay taxes on investment gains when you make withdrawals during retirement.

Roth IRA: Similar to the traditional IRA, you can put $6,000 into a Roth IRA per year. It is the most popular among the younger generation because the earnings grow tax-free. You put your after-tax dollars into this account and when you are ready to use this money, as long as the basic criteria are met, you get to enjoy that money without paying Uncle Sam.

Protecting Yourself and Others with Insurance

Insurance is about protecting yourself against a loss. Health, renters, home, auto, life, and disability insurance protect you in the event of a catastrophe. You're young and you probably feel invincible. But, having proper documents in place to protect yourself, your loved ones, and to make sure your wishes are carried out is priceless. Before you purchase any insurance, make sure you understand what is and is not covered, and also look closely at whether that type of insurance is appropriate for you.

Health Insurance: The USOC offers health insurance for those that qualify. Be mindful that though you don't pay for it out of your pocket, this insurance is taxable. You will receive a 1099 from the USOC for it each year, which you should provide to your accountant. Alternatively, you can purchase an insurance policy through private companies or by researching Affordable Care Act plans which offer subsidies depending on your income. You also have the option to be covered under your parents' insurance until age 26.

Term Life Insurance: Term life insurance is a policy you purchase at a very affordable cost, typically for 20-30 years. It is meant to protect your family during the years you are earning and accumulating wealth. The lower premium costs of term policy allows you to save and grow your wealth in other ways. The insurance benefit would only be paid out if you pass away within the term of the policy. The advantage of these policies is that they offer more protection for lower premiums during the years when you need this coverage, and it's not a bill you have to keep paying into retirement.

Permanent Life Insurance: Permanent or whole life insurance is both an insurance policy and a type of investment and wealth transfer mechanism. Premiums are paid on the policy for your whole life, instead of a set term. Part of the insurance premium will go toward the seller's commission, part toward the cost of the policy, and part will be held in a savings or investment account with the insurance company.

Because of the higher likelihood that this policy will have to pay out along with the costs mentioned above, permanent insurance is significantly more expensive than term. Seldom would a permanent policy be appropriate for a young professional. It could be something to consider if you still have money laying around after you've already completed the following:

- You have a fully funded emergency fund
- You have contributed the maximum to your retirement plan
- You have contributed to a Roth IRA

- You have set aside funds for your children's education (if that is something you want to do)

There are good people in every industry, but there are also people who are not well informed or are just plain crooked. Being a family member or close friend is not reason enough to trust that you should move forward with a life insurance purchase. Insurance should not be purchased without considering how it adds to your overall financial strategy.

Here are a few questions to ask before signing on the dotted line:

- Is this better than investing my money? Why?
- What certifications, licenses, or degrees do you have?
- What do you earn from selling me this policy vs. something cheaper?

Before you purchase, consider these things:

- Is this person thinking about my whole financial picture?
- How does this fit with my other financial goals?

You want to work with someone who is trained to review your entire financial situation, will assess all of the financial opportunities available to you, and make objective recommendations based on what's in your best interest.

Disability Insurance: Disability insurance is one of the most important types of insurance to have as a young professional because we are more likely to become disabled than to die at this time in our life. The odds of this happening increase significantly when you are a track and field athlete. Insurance companies recognize this, and as a result the premiums are quite high. This makes it tough to insure against this risk. The cost of disability insurance may be unaffordable, but it is worth looking into, and often worthwhile to pay for if you are a higher earner. For those who cannot justify the cost of the insurance premium, you should self-insure by having a significant emergency fund in the event you get injured and have to miss a season.

Estate Planning

People don't like to talk about death. It is a grim topic, but it definitely isn't easier to make tough decisions when something unexpected happens.

Frequently single young professionals do not feel there is need for estate planning documents because no one is dependent on them. However, it is better to have a plan in place that you don't have to use. Even though you are young and may not have a lot to call your own right now, you still need a plan for how things will be taken care of in the event of a tragedy. If you have a spouse or children, the need for estate planning documents is even more important.

While a comprehensive estate plan may not be necessary, having basic documents prepared in the event of incapacity is important so that your wishes are carried out. As soon as you turn eighteen, your parents are no longer your primary decision makers. If you want them to make decisions if something happens to you, you should have that documented. Having these few items in place could ensure a bad situation isn't made worse.

- A durable power of attorney is a trusted person to handle your affairs if you are unavailable or not able to make decisions for medical reasons. This can also be helpful if you need financial matters taken care of while you are overseas competing.
- A health care proxy states who can make healthcare decisions for you if you are unable to speak for yourself.

- Beneficiaries should be named on any retirement accounts or life insurance you have. This is typically required by the investment and insurance companies themselves.

- Transfer on death or payable on death can be added to your bank accounts so that once you are gone whomever you have named has access to them.

- A will states how your possessions and finances should be distributed. If no will is in place your family will have to go through the probate process which is extremely tedious. You don't want them to have to experience mountains of stress to get a couple thousand dollars out of your account. Regardless of the amount, you still would want them to have it even if just to help with the cost of wrapping up loose ends or paying for your burial services. You wouldn't want your death to create a financial strain for those you care about.

This could be a good time have a discussion with others you care about, your parents, or your spouse about whether they have estate documents in place, and setting those up if they don't. Make sure you know how to access each other's important information. You may also wish to discuss each other's wishes on whether to be buried or cremated and what you'd like your memorial service to look like.

Finding free forms online is not ideal as free often ends up costing you money in the long run. Not many people are giving away valuable, correct advice for free. Hiring an attorney to help you set up these documents is the most solid decision you can make, but the cost may be outside of your budget. A more affordable option would be an online company or legal service that will put documents together for you. That will suffice if you are young and single, but as you get older, you will likely need to add your spouse, children, property, and businesses. The more complicated your situation becomes, the more customized advice you will need. At this point, paying an attorney will be a worthwhile investment.

Earning At Various Levels

Earlier I discussed the different groups of professional athletes. While earnings vary based on event and other factors, there is some correlation between groups and types of earnings. This is how they look:

- Developing athletes' income from the sport is prize money dependent.
- Emerging elite athletes have a modest contract and depend on prize money to fill in the gaps.
- Elite athletes have sponsorship earnings large enough to support training full time and to save and plan for the future.

Athletes in each category should have a different financial strategy. Remember this is not one size fits all. Everyone's financial decisions are unique. With the charts in the following section, I will paint three different pictures outlining a possible breakdown of expenses for each: a developing, an emerging elite, and an elite athlete in order to drive home some points around the categories.

- Scenario 1 - Developing Athlete Earning $50,000 Annually
- Scenario 2 - Emerging Elite Athlete Earning $100,000 Annually
- Scenario 3 - Elite Athlete Earning $400,000 Annually

Scenario 1 - Developing Athlete Earning $50,000 Annually

You attended a school known for producing great athletes and you did well at NCAAs the final two years in college. You are determined to be a professional track athlete at any cost. You have decided to make your home in Houston because it has a great sports community and an international airport. The cost of living

CHAPTER 6 | A FINANCIAL GAME PLAN

is well below that of other cities offering the same amenities and there is no state tax. Your current income is $50,000 a year which includes $25,000 from working a part-time job and $25,000 from prize money earnings.

Explanation: To be successful at this level of competition, you need to stretch your money as far as it can go. Prize money is not paid until months after competitions, which makes you have to stretch your part time earnings. You will have to get used to paying for things that were free while you were in college. Services like physiotherapy, massages, and free equipment may no longer be available to you. As a result, paying attention to your budget and keeping your expenses low is essential to your success.

Housing: Live with roommates. You can cut your expenses significantly by sharing a place with other people. Take measures to make sure that these people are financially sound.

Agent Fee: You may not have an agent yet. If you do, $3,750-$5,000 of the money you make will go to them. The big-time agent may not have come knocking on your door, but a newer agent with less experience should be willing to work hard for you. However, be careful not to sign someone who doesn't know what they are doing simply because you don't want to do the work yourself.

50K ANNUAL BUDGET
HOUSTON, TX

EXPENSES	
Taxes	$11,000
State Taxes	$0
Agent 15%	$3,750
Physio/Medical	$900
Travel	$4,000
Equipment	$1,000
Coaching	$150
Housing	$9,600
Food	$6,000
Fun/Other	$2,000
Accountant	$350
Cert. Financial Planner	$750
SAVINGS	
Emergency Saving	$5,000
Life After Sport Savings	$0
Retierment Savings	$5,500
Add'l Savings Goals	$0
TOTAL	**$50,000**

Medical Expenses: If you can, get free services (physiotherapy, massages, and chiropractic care) from a university or a massage school. That will help your budget quite a bit. Otherwise you may be limited to one massage a month and physiotherapy when it's necessary for performance. Consider these services as a luxury until you are making enough money to pay all your expenses.

Travel Budget: You will need to work hard to find affordable flights, ask for help from loved ones, and even find creative ways to cover expenses. You will not make money if you cannot get to a race to perform.

Equipment: You will have to purchase workout clothes, a competition uniform, shoes, and other equipment necessary to compete. Do not hesitate to ask someone for their hand me downs. Humility will keep your budget in line.

Coaching: You are probably being coached by someone who is hoping to see you succeed. You will not have money to pay them right now, but as you grow you will find opportunities to return the favor. This is usually your high school or college coach who has a special place in their heart for you. Buy them a few meals to show your appreciation.

Accountant and Financial Planner: You can do a short-term engagement with a financial planner for about $750 to get your finances on the right track. That is 1.5% of what you make. Isn't it worth 1.5% to make sure you are being responsible with the other 98.5%? You will also want to hire an accountant to help you with your taxes. There are so many rules for professional athletes that spending money to have an accountant ensures you don't miss anything on your taxes can save you hundreds or thousands of dollars.

Savings: Start building your emergency fund. It might not be much, but you need money for a rainy day. By saving 10% over 12 months, you will have your first $5,000 saved. The goal is to have $15,000 saved in order to have a strong emergency fund.

Scenario 2 - Emerging Elite Athlete Earning $100,000 Annually

You have a contract that allows you to train full time but you are by no means "ballin." You are not scraping by financially, but because you get free gear and train full time, your friends and family may assume your earnings are larger than they are. Your current income is $100,000 a year, which includes $60,000 from a shoe contract and $40,000 from prize money. Your $60,000 is paid quarterly and prize money trickles in months after the money has been earned. You have a full competition schedule with both domestic and international competitions. You have chosen to live in Arizona because it is affordable and you can train in various conditions; however, you are paying a state tax.

Explanation: You make more than most of your friends that are working a 9-5 job. Your office is not a cramped desk in a cubicle and your schedule has flexibility and includes travel on someone else's dime. This is a good life. You don't want the stress of poor money management keeping you from focusing on furthering your career. You can save, live, and use some of your earnings to have some fun.

100K ANNUAL BUDGET
SCOTTSDALE, AZ

EXPENSES	
Taxes	$24,000
State Taxes	$3,400
Agent 15%	$9,000
Physio/Medical	$2,000
Travel	$4,000
Equipment	$500
Coaching	$5,000
Housing	$12,000
Food	$7,000
Fun/Other	$4,000
Accountant	$800
Cert. Financial Planner	$2,400

SAVINGS	
Emergency Saving	$10,000
Life After Sport Savings	$5,000
Retierment Savings	$10,000
Add'l Savings Goals	$900
TOTAL	**$100,000**

Housing: You can rent an apartment on your own, but a money maven would still get roommates. Finding like-minded people to share your living space will help your career and your wallet.

Agent Fee: You are paying your agent the standard 15-20%. This amounts to $15,000-$20,000.

Medical Expenses: You have scheduled physiotherapy and massages every other week and pay $75 per visit when traveling. This is routine maintenance.

Travel Budget: You will have a small travel budget through your contract, but you still have to contribute and choose wisely. Now traveling involves bringing your coach along and paying their way. A single room at a meet isn't a given. If you arrive at the hotel and don't like your roommate, you'll have to pay extra to get a private room. This will increase your travel costs.

Equipment: Congratulations! Your sponsor covers equipment and uniforms, but you get a 1099 every year for that. You will have to pay taxes on these things as if it was income.

Coaching: You may still be coached by someone hoping to see you succeed. However, you can probably afford to pay something. If your coach doesn't ask you to pay, consider giving them a monetary gift at the end of the season after you have done the final accounting of your finances. It is also tax deductible and the right thing to do. Your coach has given you their time all year long. Their contribution helped you perform and earn the funds you now have. Show appreciation monetarily when you are able to pay them.

Accountant and Financial Planner: These expenses are essential. You can expect to pay around $2,400 for a financial planner to work with you on an ongoing basis and $800 for an accountant.

Savings: You should be able to save at least 20% of your annual income. Depending on where you are in your career this will be distributed between an emergency fund, a "life after sports" savings account, and your retirement savings.

Scenario 3 - Elite Athlete Earning $400,000 Annually

In this scenario, you have chosen to live in Atlanta because of the amenities the city has to offer and the low cost of living. You have decided to buy a home instead of renting. Your agent is working hard for you and you have recently hired a talent/Public Relations (PR) agent in order to boost your appeal and handle your social media. You have a personal massage therapist who travels with you, and for big events you also take your physiotherapist.

Explanation: You have made it! You are the best of the best in the track and field industry. As an athlete who makes $400,000 a year, you are one of the sport's elites. You have a $250,000 shoe contract, make $100,000 in prize money, and earned $50,000 from additional sponsorship opportunities your PR agent secured for you. The biggest mistake you can make is choosing to not spend money on services that will bring value to your business. A sponsor has invested this money in you with the expectation that you will

400K ANNUAL BUDGET
ATLANTA, GA

EXPENSES	
Taxes	$124,000
State Taxes	$23,000
Agent 15%	$52,500
PR Agency	$10,000
Physio/Medical	$7,000
Travel	$0
Equipment	$0
Coaching	$30,000
Housing	$24,000
Food	$10,000
Fun/Other	$7,500
Accountant	$1,500
Cert. Financial Planner	$4,000
SAVINGS	
Emergency Saving	$40,000
Life After Sport Savings	$30,000
Retierment Savings	$30,000
Add'l Savings Goals	$6,500
TOTAL	**$400,000**

invest in ways that will help you perform your best. It hurts writing checks to your team (your coach, agent, accountant, physiotherapist, etc.), but without them the risk of your performance diminishing is significant.

The temptation will be to "go big" in spending on fun things (e.g. cars, jewelry/watches, clothes, and gadgets) because now you can afford it. Resist this urge! A track and field career is short, but within it you have the potential to set yourself up for financial freedom for your lifetime.

Housing: Don't overdo it here. Your inclination may be to get a pimped-out home, and the real estate agent and mortgage broker will say, "Yes, do it! You're approved." You may qualify for a hefty mortgage payment right now, but remember the mortgage is spread over 30 years. Even if you have an awesome and long 10-year career (which very few do) you still have 20 years left to pay on this house after sports. What job will allow you to pay the same amount on your mortgage each month when you are done competing? Do not forget about the expenses associated with home ownership. Furnishing, landscaping, and maintenance (the things no one ever plans for) can break the bank. When thinking about the cost of housing, think long term.

Agent Fee: You are paying your agent the standard 15-20%. This amounts to $52,500-$70,000.

Talent/PR Agent: Next level performance and next level earning require next level branding to maximize opportunities and other endorsement deals. Expect to pay 20% for deals secured on your behalf by a talent/PR agent.

Medical Expenses: Someone paid you big money for big performances. To perform you need to be healthy. Your medical team is now part of your "staff." You have a small stipend from your sponsor but it doesn't cover everything you need to stay healthy, so you pay out of pocket for a medical team to work with you and travel with you, which adds a significant amount of money to the expenses in this category.

Travel Budget: You will probably have a nice travel budget and most meets will pay for your travel. A possible expense you will incur will be upgrades on flights, not because you are high-maintenance, but because you need to recover as quickly as possible. You can use these funds to get a single room at a meet that only offers roommates, and other members of your staff's travel expenses may also fall into this category.

Equipment: Your sponsor covers equipment and uniforms. You might get to have a few "custom" pieces or have shoes that are custom fitted. Enjoy the perks but don't forget you get a 1099 every year for those items as part of your income.

Coaching: You are paying your coach's salary and for them to travel with you. You make $400,000 and they make $30,000. Do you see why there are training groups? Coaches need 15 athletes to earn a living as good as yours. Meanwhile your agent has made at least $52,000. This is why coaches are starting to band together.

Accountant and Financial Planner: You need to have someone who is as concerned with your financial future as you are. These expenses are essential at this level. At this earning level your taxes will be high and strategies for saving and being tax efficient will be key for you being able to keep more of the funds for yourself. Your financial planning needs are more complex than most people's and there are various strategies to maximize your earnings. Expect to pay at least $4,000 a year to receive high quality customized advice.

Savings: You should be saving at least 20% of your annual income. If you are a next-level thinker you will be saving more, only living off of your contract, and stacking away all your prize money and endorsement earnings. You should also be contributing to a "life after sports" account and retirement savings. After all of this, you should still have money left over.

Building Your Financial Team

We all come from different financial backgrounds. Some grew up in families that never discussed money, while others grew up in households that talked constantly about creating wealth and being financially responsible. Maybe you came from a family that doesn't have a lot of financial literacy. Maybe your parents had terrible spending habits and complained about how hard things were because there wasn't enough money. No matter what your background is, you have the ability to make good decisions with your finances and change the messages you heard. Starting new money behavior begins with recognizing that you don't know everything and valuing the advice of an expert.

While we all can manage our finances on our own, it does not mean we should. Your team may begin with coaches and teammates, but there is a big network of people who will be supporting you on your journey. Some will be people you've known your whole life while others will be people you interview and put under scrutiny to make sure they are the best fit for you. When interviewing any of the professionals you want to hire, you are always looking to learn about three things: personality, services, and cost/fees.

Personality can be tricky. While you want someone relatable, you don't want someone that is all charisma and not very knowledgeable. It may be hard to communicate with "Nerdy Nate," but at the end of the day your business will be done right. It would be good to be able to find a good mix of both: someone who can break things down in a way that you can understand, but is also well-versed in their work. You need to find this balance to feel set up for success.

Services will vary and the options are not one size fits all. Think about what you feel like you need and make a list of those things before heading into a meeting with the professional. This is important so you are not just sold on what the person is offering without carefully considering whether your needs will be met.

Costs and fees will be different among professionals, just like for your coach and agent. The method in which they are paid will also vary from hourly, to monthly retainers, to one lump sum. It is important that you get multiple perspectives and quotes for financial services so that you are aware of what is possible. Don't base your decision about someone solely on cost. The cheapest option at the beginning could be more costly in the long run. If you hire a novice who is charging less to get their business going, you may end up paying a price to give them experience. It could be that the individual who charges more works more efficiently and knows the system because they have done it for years. It is important to value the service you are receiving and make the appropriate investment so that the job is done right.

Taxes and Hiring an Accountant

All the money you receive, unfortunately is not yours. There are two certainties in life: death and taxes! We all owe some of our money to the United States government. Our dollars are used to fund Social Security, Medicare and Medicaid, welfare programs, national security, veteran support, transportation, and education. It is not fun to give away a hefty portion of your earnings without having a real say as to how it is used. But you and some of your loved ones will likely reap the benefits of one of these programs at some point. Try to focus on the good it can do instead of what it may or may not be doing for you right now. We don't have to like it, but we do need to abide by it.

Uncle Sam does not send you a bill with an envelope to send in your payment. That is not how taxes work. You are responsible for setting aside, calculating, and paying your taxes on time, every year. This is why you should consider hiring an accountant.

Failure to file and pay taxes is one of the biggest obstacles athletes face. Being disorganized and making assumptions about how much will be owed without any professional number crunching is a recipe for disaster. Do not listen to your friend who says you don't have to file because you don't make enough. And unless they are a Certified Public Accountant (CPA) or an Enrolled Agent (EA), don't let your family member file for you, even if they do their own taxes and everyone else's in the family. Many people who prepare taxes are not CPAs or an EA. In fact, just about anyone can pay a small fee and register for a Preparer Tax Identification Number (PTIN) and start doing taxes.

Not paying taxes or setting aside enough of what you earn frequently derails a professional athlete's finances. A good accountant will tell you how much you should be setting aside for taxes and also identify legitimate ways you can reduce the amount of tax dollars you pay. The accountant you hire should be knowledgeable about your specific business environment. Tax planning is where you can implement strategies to save money and continue to build wealth.

Professional athletes have unique write-offs. Whether you are trying to make ends meet or earning plenty, the accounting for participation in track and field needs to be excellent. I have seen a very modest earner be audited and told that they were not participating in the sport as a profession, but instead as a hobby. They had to defend themselves and prove that they were in fact participating in the sport to earn a living. The IRS may mistake you for the person who is training for a marathon for fun, but you are not and you need to have someone who can defend you if they were to make claims like this, and better yet prevent them from seeing anything that would have them make a claim like this in the first place. A Certified Public Accountant (CPA) or an Enrolled Agent (EA) can represent you if you are audited.

An accountant will analyze things such as:

- Whether or not it makes sense for you to become an LLC or incorporate
- Whether you should be paying yourself a salary
- How much you should set aside for taxes on a quarterly basis
- Whether you would benefit from bookkeeping services

If your earnings are low, look into the USOC resource as a way to get your taxes done for free or inexpensively. On the website *www.the-oval-office.com* I have also provided links to tax resources.

When you do find someone to do your taxes, come prepared. Don't show up with a shoebox of receipts; there are apps for that. The less time your accountant has to spend on getting you organized, the lower your fees will be. Time is money, so you need to be sure you aren't wasting either. You may wish to call ahead of time and ask what will be needed at your tax appointment.

Financial Planning Professionals

One of the hardest things to navigate when looking for financial advice is knowing what sort of professional you need. I wish there was an easy way to paint this picture, but unfortunately there are various titles and just as many services when looking for financial help. The terms used in this world are very muddled. Anyone can wake up in the morning and call themselves a:

- Financial Advisor
- Financial Coach
- Financial Planner
- Financial Consultant
- Wealth Manager
- Investment Manager

The only thing someone cannot call themselves without making a false claim is a CERTIFIED FINANCIAL PLANNER™ professional (CFP®). CFP® certification is the highest standard there is in the financial industry. There is an education requirement, comprehensive exam, minimum amount of experience, and a code of ethics CFP® professionals are bound to.

My recommendation is to only work with someone who is a CFP® professional, but no matter who you choose make sure you do your due diligence in selecting someone to help you. This is hard when you don't know what you don't know. Ask questions. You are paying them to help you, so ask all the questions you want. Avoid those who focus more on being your friend than the business they are doing for you. If you aren't happy with the financial professional you choose after you start working with them, know that you are free to end the business relationship with them and choose someone else.

When interviewing a potential financial professional here are some questions you should ask them:

- **What licenses and/or designations do you have? What does that qualify you to do?** Not all financial professionals have the same educational background, professional experience, and/or designations. Answers to this question may vary but it is important to ask for more details.

- **How familiar are you with my unique needs?** Check to

see if there is someone that best suits your unique financial needs. Some financial professionals may have expertise in a particular area. Does this person focus on clients in a particular profession (e.g. doctors, real estate agents, athletes, etc.)? Is there a particular age group that they work with? Do they have a specialty (e.g. student loan debt, stock options, or families with children with disabilities)? No question is a dumb one. Be sure to ask about the things that matter most to you.

- **What does your investment management entail?** This will give you an overview this financial professional's investment philosophy. A good follow-up question if the answer isn't clear is, "Do you believe in an active or passive investment approach?"

- **How do you charge? How do you get paid? What is the cost of your services?** These questions are similar, but different, so you will want to ask all three. Some advisors will try to make it seem as if their services are free, but when you dig deeper they are not. For example, their earnings may be hidden in fees automatically taken when you choose to invest in certain funds. It is important to know what you will be paying so there are no surprises down the road. The National Association of Personal Financial Advisors (NAPFA), has divided compensation into three categories:

  - **Fee-Only Compensation:** This model minimizes conflicts of interest. A fee-only financial advisor charges the client directly for his or her advice and/or ongoing management. No other financial reward is provided by any institution, which means that the advisor does not receive commissions on the actions they take on their client's behalf. Compensation is based on an hourly rate, a percent of assets managed, a flat fee, or a retainer.

  - **Fee-Based Compensation** (fee and commission):

This form is often confused with fee-only, but it's not the same. Fee-based advisors charge clients a fee for the advice delivered, but they also sometimes receive payments for products they sell or recommend. In some cases, commissions are credited towards the fee, giving the appearance of a lower-priced option, but any outside compensation lessens the advisor's ability to keep the client's best interests first and foremost.

○ **Commission:** Commissioned advisors are paid a commission for financial products sold. It is sometime unclear what you are being charged for their services. A client working with a commissioned salesperson must always ask himself: Is this advice truly in my best interest, or is it the most profitable product for the advisor? Unfortunately, often the answer is the latter. In fact, a commissioned advisor usually is required to put the best interests of his employer ahead of the best interests of his client.

• **Are you a fiduciary?** Not all financial professionals are fiduciaries. A fiduciary has a legal obligation to act in your best interest. This obligation eliminates conflict of interest concerns and makes a fiduciary's advice more trustworthy. I recommend only working with fiduciaries.

I believe that it is important to have written financial goals. People who plan, put their goals in writing, and regularly check in on those goals have a higher likelihood of success and personal fulfillment. A solid financial plan encourages you to reflect on your values and goals and incorporate them both on your path towards financial stability and independence.

Money is emotional. There is a lot that goes into organizing your finances, so don't be cheap when it comes to hiring a financial professional now just to be broke in the future. Don't just earn and spend it. Earn, save, then spend.

PRO TIP 👍 DASHING FOR DOLLARS

As a professional athlete, I got into a pattern where I would see a crossbar and know if I cleared it, it was worth $2,000. Every single time I stepped to the line, I thought about the financial implications. It was an ugly way to pole vault. After 2004, I made a commitment to myself that I would only be performing for the sake of performance and not for the financial gain. It was an intentional choice that I am so glad I made.

When I realized performance drives everything and the money would follow me, it took the pressure off money-making and I could start to enjoy the process of competing again. When I was just seeking money, money didn't come. It was a valuable lesson. Go after your performance and the money will follow you. That is the right order to concentrate on. You have the God-given ability. Do everything in your power to be your best, rise to the occasion, and to put your talents on display - not just to get a paycheck.

Brad Walker
IAAF World Championships gold medalist, pole vault

CHAPTER 7

BRANDING

---

*"Your career sustains you now. Your brand sustains you for
the rest of your life."*

- Ato Boldon, four-time Olympic Medalist

As athletes, we must consider how we present ourselves to the world. Building a brand requires a balance between your authentic self and the person the world sees. It matters how the world sees you, especially when you are representing more than just yourself. However, it also matters that you are comfortable being you and not just putting on a show to please others.

You need to establish the narrative around your brand. Some athletes desire fame and want to share their story, while others are focused on competing and believe that good performances will provide them with the platform they desire. While performing well is generally part of the criteria, it is not the only requirement for building a profitable brand. You can win and still not get a single endorsement. Branding is about your ability to tell your story in a dynamic way.

There are many aspects of creating a strong brand. We think of social media as being the primary approach, but there is so much more to creating a platform to positively portray yourself. Let's start with your appearance.

Appearance

Because we are in sports, there isn't really an expectation for us to wear a glamorous, dressed to the nines wardrobe. Yet, we sometimes get too relaxed. How you choose to present and carry yourself both during and after competitions may dictate the opportunities available to you. It is important to be thinking about the way you dress and to take care of your physical appearance.

Track and field athletes have great bodies and frequently compete in skimpy outfits. If you want a professional image, skip the skimpy athletic gear and choose to wear clothing that expresses a different side of you. You may even get extra publicity because you are wearing unique and modest apparel. Two athletes who have done this well are Allyson Felix and Sanya Richards-Ross. They have shown that you can be beautiful without sexualizing yourself.

You also should be mindful of the expected dress code at the various events you attend. When you go to a business meeting, dress in business attire. When you know you'll be interviewed on camera (not directly after you compete), dress sharp. If you're not sure what is expected, it is better to be overdressed than to be underdressed.

Your warm up clothes shouldn't be what you leave the house in if you're not actually going to practice. Old sweats that fit poorly and look as if you just finished working out are not a look that will attract opportunities. Keep your public appearance in mind when you go out and think about what you want to wear on camera when you shop for clothes. You never know who might be watching.

Everyone has a distinct style and we are all attracted to a variety of fashions. It is wonderful to have so many options. You get to choose your look, but know your audience. Tattoos and colorful hair will attract an audience different than a business suit and slacks. No matter the genre of clothing and hairstyle, you should be clean and put together. Whether you intend for it to happen or not, you will most likely be a role model for other aspiring athletes and young people, and that is a high calling.

If you are not truly into fashion this takes effort. It is easy to find sexy and frumpy, but the in-between is a little harder. It could be worth hiring a personal stylist to help you look your best on and off the track. Dress professionally because believe me, when the track opportunities run out or your body simply wears out, you will need to get another job and employers don't look fondly on people who wear sweats with holes in the knees and oversized t-shirts. Consider this an investment in both your present and future job opportunities.

Behavior

The news consistently highlights athletes getting arrested, embarrassing their sponsors and country, and living as if the world revolves around them and as if there are no consequences for their actions. They forget that they are public figures who represent something bigger than themselves. One unprofessional decision can cause irreparable damage or even end your career.

Remember that when you travel to compete, you are in the spotlight and you are at work. I've seen time and time again athletes who party hard with the locals after meets are over. Some even miss their flights because they are hungover, and then expect the meet promoters to pay to change their flight home.

Having a good time in your work environment is acceptable; you should be having fun. Having fun doesn't mean that alcohol or other substances need to be involved. To be successful, you need to establish boundaries and have self-control. If you lose control because of alcohol or drugs, your sponsors may distance themselves from you because your poor behavior damages their brand.

Here are a few ways you can maintain a professional image while on the road competing:

- Gauge your surroundings, and act as if your sponsor, the meet director, and your grandmother are next to you seeing what you are doing. What would they think of you representing them in that way?

- When having alcohol in a work setting, limit consumption to two drinks. Getting drunk in public is embarrassing and inappropriate behavior. You can celebrate without getting inebriated.

- Pay your bills. You are responsible for paying your tabs and any costs incurred at your expense. For example, if you go to a restaurant and run up a tab, you need to be prepared to pay for it and not expect someone else to cover it.

I chose to not drink at all when I was on the road, and I still had a great time! I enjoyed having dinner with friends and touring the towns we were in. Just being with people and exploring new cities was fun for me.

The Oral and Written Word

How were your grades in your English and public speaking classes? Regardless of how well you did in school, how you speak and write matters. Brand sponsors are looking for individuals who can clearly articulate their message to their audience and represent them well. Text messages with abbreviations and silly emojis are okay to use with friends and family, but when you are communicating via email or text with others outside of your close circle, you should eliminate the use of emojis and make an effort to double check the spelling, punctuation, and grammar in your message before you hit send. Likewise, some slang speech is okay in a personal social setting, but if you want to be a spokesperson for a large company they will want you to speak well both in conversations, media interviews, and in front of large groups. They are expecting you to influence those around you and be a professional.

Having a camera shoved in your face a few seconds after competing and still breathing hard is not ideal, but it comes with the territory. Media training offered by the USATF and USOC is something worth investing in if you want to handle the media attention in a way that is going to expand your platform. Here are some tips for dealing with the media.

- Be careful what you say out loud, whether in an interview or on social media. You are always on the record.

- Always be aware of who is interviewing you. It is good to learn reporters' names and greet them with their names because they appreciate being seen as a person and that connection could make them more fond of speaking to you and writing about you. It is also important to know that all reporters are not your friends and to beware of Negative Nate.

- Understand the difference between a softball and a landmine. The reporter could be fair or completely biased.

Softball example: "Jane, are you the happiest silver medalist ever?" This is very easy to answer. Landmine example: "Hey Jane, why does the U.S. drop the stick so much?" No matter how you answer, what you say will be scrutinized.

- Practice responding to controversial questions that may be directed to you.

- You are allowed to redirect the conversation. If someone asks you something you aren't comfortable answering, just redirect the question by focusing on your particular event and the outcome. For example, if you just won the shot put a reporter may ask you, "Why did the men drop the baton?" Don't be afraid to say, "While it is unfortunate that they didn't have success, I am really excited to have just won my competition and am happy to answer any questions about that."

- Speak firmly and make eye contact. Do not mumble. You need to speak with confidence and authority without being overbearing or pushy.

- Don't speak ill about your competitors or the winner. No one likes a sore loser. Be gracious. Show sportsmanship all the time.

Social Media Success

In addition to traditional media, you now have the ability to share as much or as little as you want via social media platforms. Whether you love it or hate it, social media is not going away. Right now, there is no better way share your brand than by having a consistent social media presence. Engaging your audience with thoughtful, creative, and interesting content is important. Here are some things to remember regarding social media:

- Don't bash companies/organizations on social media,

especially if you have a personal issue with them. When you are frustrated about something, ask yourself, "Who can I talk to about this? Have I reached out to these people directly?" Sending an email is fine, but an unanswered email is not a reason to vent your frustration on social media. Give the person a call. Leave a voicemail, but without the angry rant. You do not want to share the details of your frustration because it is recorded. Reach out to multiple points of contact on an issue to pursue resolution.

- ◦ For example, in the case of a late paycheck or not being admitted to the national championships when you think you have the right mark, take the time to reach out to the pertinent USATF staff member, then reach out to the AAC. Your emergency is not necessarily everyone else's emergency. Be patient and wait for a response.

- Social media is great, but business by Snapchat only is not a good way to go. Respond to emails and answer calls. Remember you are a professional.

- If a picture is worth 1,000 words, a video is worth 10,000. Visual content is taking priority over written content. There are fancy algorithms that will prioritize visual content so those posts will get more engagement.

- Decide which platform is best for you and focus your attention there. You don't have to be active on every social media platform to make an impact.

- Posting several times a day is a lot of work. Posting thoughtful content two to three times a week should be plenty.

- Be authentic. Choose to post about what matters to you, not what you think will get the most engagement. This will get rid of followers who don't share the same interests as you and will also attract people who love you for who you are.

- You can be a private person and have a public brand. It is possible to do both. Decide what you are comfortable sharing. People don't want to just know your image or persona, they want to know you. Let them in at a level that you feel is appropriate.

- Sharing a link that takes your followers away from the platform will have a negative impact on engagement. For example, Facebook wants users on Facebook, so if you send them to your blog via a link to your website expect it to be seen a little less.

- Give shout outs to others. People love to receive positive remarks and comments and are likely to follow you or share your posts when you interact with them on social media regularly. Learn to use hashtags and tag other people relevant to the post. It will help your post reach more people and increase the likelihood of those people sharing the post on their page or reposting. This is a great free way to increase followers and get more interaction with your page.

- Ignore, block, or unfriend people who post nasty comments. It is not a worthwhile endeavor to engage with a mean person who has 60 followers. Some people are mad for no reason and you can't let them bring you down. They might just hate the team you are on or the entire country you're from. You cannot let this take up your time.

- Get off social media when you are heading into a big event so you can be focused and ready to perform your best. You can send out a message that says what you want it to say, but don't get distracted by scrolling through other posts and don't wait around for likes or comments. There is actually a feature where you can turn off comments. Sometimes you don't need people's opinion of your picture.

Social media can contribute to your advancement or to your downfall; it is really up to you.

Educate Yourself About the Industry

Staying aware of the issues and the current news in the event you compete in and the industry surrounding it is important. You must know what's going on around you and how you fit into the picture. The various organizations relevant to track and field have robust websites full of information you need to succeed. They also are available to follow on every social media platform.

PRO TIP 👍

Follow these organizations on social media:

- IAAF International Association of Athletics Federations
- WADA World Anti-Doping Agency
- USADA United States Anti-Doping Agency
- USATF USA Track and Field
- AAC Athletes' Advisory Committee
- AIU Athletics Integrity Unit

The Importance of Having a Website and Professional Photos

Having a personal website is yet another way to take control of sharing your story with fans and possible sponsors. There are elaborate sites that do all sorts of things, but there are also cost efficient templates that will have you up and running in just a couple of hours. If you want a quality free option AthleteBiz offers free beautiful websites for athletes to tell their story. You will hear "content is king," but posting new content takes an investment of time. If this is not an area you're interested in, then create some content that is timeless and does not require much upkeep.

Think of your website as your virtual resume.

- The "About" section should showcase your story and accomplishments, both athletic and non-sports related. Some people will read this verbatim when introducing you at speaking engagements. Write a bio that illustrates how you want to be portrayed, and have someone help you if needed. Set up an automatic reminder for yourself to go into this section after every season and take an hour to update it.

- Make sure the "Contact" section has accurate and up-to-date information so that people can reach you or your designated representative. Don't assume people know your coach, agent, or manager and can find you through them.

- If you link to Wikipedia, double check its accuracy and that it says what you want the world to know about you. If it is not accurate, you can simply go in and hit the edit button to make corrections.

You will want to post various pictures of you on and off the track on your website. Finding action shots can be tricky. Hundreds of photographers may snap your picture while you are competing and you have no right to them. There are some nice photographers that will share those photos with you for free, but in general you are going to need to purchase the photos. It is unfortunate that you could end your career and not have a single professional picture of you competing to use on your website or social media profile without paying hundreds of dollars.

To avoid this, consider hiring a photographer to capture some action shots of you at one or two meets. You can find a local affordable photographer where your meet will be held pretty easily now using various apps for freelancers (Craigslist, Thumbtack, TaskRabbit, etc.). This would be much more cost effective than paying $700 for one picture with limited rights later on. I regret not having done this during my career. Finding a good photographer to document your career in the way that best represents you will be priceless.

Timing Matters

Some athletes think, "If I can just make this team, everything will be different," but that is not necessarily the case. When brands are looking for an athlete to attach themselves to for the Olympics, they start looking well in advance. There is a large media summit and promo shoot that happens a year in advance. If you have been identified as an Olympic hopeful, USATF and NBC will invite you to go. They hold this media summit so that they have tons of cool footage and interviews before the Olympics. This means they are choosing the ambassadors based on the previous year's performance or your potential to medal.

When the Olympic Games are over, the marketing draw has also come to an end for big sponsors. How well the media told your story will largely determine what you receive as compensation in the future. If you are not the chosen story, opportunities may be limited. There will be opportunities when you have great performances, but they might not be as plentiful or as substantial as what you had in mind. You aren't completely powerless however; there are some things you can control.

Sponsors want to see you being respectful. Being too quiet with no personality or too loud and obnoxious can be detrimental to your image. Closed mouths don't get fed; loud mouths generally don't either. Find the middle ground.

Two exceptions I can think of are Maurice Greene and Allyson Felix. Maurice was a nice guy you always knew was in a room because you could hear his booming voice and reverberating laughter before you could see him. The second is Allyson Felix, who has spent most of her career being seen but not heard. She is the most decorated athlete in the history of the sport. Showing up and winning as consistently as she does doesn't require much to be said. However, I wouldn't bank on being silent and letting your performance do the talking for you because your performances may not be so consistently stellar to keep you in the spotlight for your whole career. Allyson is a special athlete.

On the opposite side, I would not take the approach that the squeaky wheel gets the grease. You risk being labeled obnoxious and narcissistic, causing people to flee when they see you coming because they cannot stand the sound of your voice anymore. Instead, find the balance that most resonates with who you are.

PRO TIP 👍 A WORD OF WARNING

At times, platforms you earn can become a distraction. A friend of mine became pretty high profile. One year she was flying here and there for TV shows and other appearances. Some places didn't have a track for her to train. She didn't have a great season and she confided in me after a race that her performance wasn't stellar because of an inconsistent training schedule.

Being famous and traveling for appearances can be a slippery slope leading to skipped workouts. Factor in travel time when considering how it will affect your training schedule and ask your hosts if there will be gyms or tracks available nearby. There are only so many workouts you can do in a hotel gym and still be truly staying in shape to perform well.

Networking As Part of Your Brand

Like any business owner, you will need to learn how to network with people. You will meet many amazing people during your career. Your training partners will be your friends for life, but don't exclude yourself from non-athletes. They can expose you to different cultural experiences and circles of influence. Tune in to who they are and get to know them.

If you go to a party or event and you want to enter the conversation with a circle of people, simply ask, "May I join you?" Talking about sports will be an easy conversation starter, but when you don't want to talk about sports any longer, you can redirect the conversation to ask what the other people in the group are passionate about. Ask a lot of questions. Most people love to talk about themselves.

After you exchange contact info, you will want to follow up and tell them it was nice to meet them and reach out to offer items of value every so often based on what you know about them. It could be as simple as sharing a link to an article on a subject that they mentioned they are passionate about. When you nurture the relationship and stay in touch, you show them you are genuinely interested in them and not just positioning yourself for an opportunity. You never know who may need your help or whose help you will need at some point in the future.

Branding in the Community

Volunteering and doing community service are important parts of your overall brand. Corporations love seeing athletes doing positive work in their communities. Besides that, it's the right thing to do to give back. Find something you're passionate about and give your time, talents, and (if you're able) your treasure (money) to that cause. Donating your time to speak to younger athletes or help at a camp could create a lifelong connection. Sometimes you may be asked to give to a cause. Even giving $15 to the cause will be appreciated. No amount is too small when it is genuine.

While your main goal should be to think about what you can give and not what you can get, don't underestimate how building relationships early in your career could result in opportunities to find resources in your future. Community service is a great way to network as well as give back.

You have been given a unique platform as an athlete. Make time to give back. Stopping to sign a autograph or answer a question can inspire someone to keep going. You never know when someone is being influenced by you. You may not be able to see them, but they see you and often remember your behavior. Maybe one day, you'll learn you've had such a positive impact that people name their kids after you. There's a reason there are tons of Kobes and LeBrons and Serenas out there. I have even met a few girls named "Lauryn" over the years and feel honored that people would name their child after me. The legacy you leave behind is going to be more meaningful than any amount of money you will earn or medal you will win.

Professional Help

While there is much you can do to build you own brand. You may also want to consider enlisting the help of a talent/Public Relations (PR) agent for you. In the same way we have discussed your doing due diligence in hiring in other areas, you will also need to be cautious in finding a talent/PR agent. Be careful of the self-proclaimed PR expert who is selling you a social media platform, fancy business cards, and promising you the world. You must ask questions and give people a chance to prove themselves.

If someone is newer to the industry, set up compensation in such a way that they only get paid when they perform, versus an agreement to pay them out of pocket on a recurring basis with no evidence that a strategy is in fact being implemented. Most PR agents will charge a standard fee of 20% of any deal they get for you. I recommend paying like this on a percentage basis instead of on a regular basis so that you will both benefit when they procure additional earnings for you. Be clear about what they are providing and make sure that is in line with your expectations.

Understand that you're the CEO and president of your brand. Therefore, you decide the kind of success you want to attain as an athlete. To be a successful professional, it requires your 100 percent commitment on and off the track.

CHAPTER 8

NUTRITION, SUPPLEMENTS, & DOPING

"I put my trust in someone and was let down. If I could do everything all over again, I definitely would do things differently."

-Tyson Gay, 100m IAAF World Champions and American record holder

As I write this book, we are in the midst of one of the most trying times sports have ever faced from a doping perspective. Russia ran a sponsored doping program and it ruined grand moments for hundreds of athletes. It has left a cloud on Olympic sports and scarred many professional athletes for life. The handling of such a widespread scandal was poor.

Russia took advantage of hosting the 2014 Winter Olympics in their country by swapping dirty urine samples with clean ones for their athletes, but Russian athletes were still allowed to compete in the 2016 Olympics. They were then granted permission to compete in the 2018 Winter Olympics under a neutral flag that was not neutral at all. Shortly after the Games, they were reinstated as a country and have already been allowed to have major competitions on their home soil again. As disgraceful as the system is, there are still rules, and while they don't seem to apply to everyone, you can be certain they apply to American athletes as well as track and field athletes all over the world.

No matter how good or bad the system is, the system does not govern your personal integrity. If you think cheating is an option, quit now! This is never a happy topic to address when it comes to going pro. If you think you will not be approached to make a career-altering decision to try a new supplement or dope like other young, vulnerable, and talented athletes, you're wrong. It's everywhere and in many forms.

In 2004, I won the silver medal in the Olympics. I was twenty years old and had just come out of college. I opened my cupboard in off-season and saw bottles of pills. Our coach had given us multivitamin and fish oil pills under a common brand name. I never took those pills. I wasn't disciplined and just didn't care to take them. I was a kid. Every time my teammates said they were running low on vitamins, I figured I had better say I was, too. That is why I had a cupboard full of them! I had won a silver medal without them.

In my mind you're either naturally gifted or you're not; however science is not pointless. I think it can be used to help you better understand how to optimize what is inside of you. For instance, if your blood test results say you have low vitamin D, you can eat foods high in that vitamin. As a professional, I wouldn't just pop a vitamin D pill. I would do my homework and invest in myself by researching what foods I should eat or other things I could do to naturally increase my vitamin D levels, like getting more sun.

If you have confidence in your natural ability, there will be no need to take pills and supplements. I was supplement-free my whole career.

I am a four-time Olympian who earned three medals. I know this won't discourage everyone from using supplements, so I am going to give you additional information from the sports authorities.

USADA (United States Anti-Doping Agency) is the national anti-doping organization in the U.S. for Olympic, Paralympic, & Pan American Sports Games, with the job of protecting clean athletes and the integrity of sports. U.S. athletes who are designated as part of the testing pool are required to submit information on their whereabouts and be available for testing. This is part of the job just like training and competing. Neglecting this responsibility can negatively impact your career.

Athletes are subject to a huge invasion of privacy to do what we love. Sample collection can happen during competitions or outside of competitions. If you earn a medal you can expect to be tested. Testers can show up at your house early in the morning or they might show up at the track while you are practicing. If they show up and you are headed out to grab dinner with friends, you can have them follow you to the restaurant or tell your friends you will catch up with them after you pee in a cup at home. Is it inconvenient? Yes. However, it comes with the right to compete at such a high level.

It is important to know both your responsibility and your rights. Here is an overview of what to expect when you're competing as a professional athlete.

Whereabouts: You are required to let USADA know where you are at all times so that they can find you for drug testing. This is not a typo. You need to fill out forms sharing your whereabouts with the USADA quarterly and on time. Filling out these forms is your responsibility not your agents' or your parents' responsibility. Don't get complacent because a missed test will have you sitting on the sideline unable to compete and unable to earn a living.

Sample collection: The process of collecting urine samples is a complete invasion of your personal space and loss of all your privacy. You may be asked to take your pants down, pull your shirt up, and spin around in a circle to make sure there are no devices on you that you could use to cheat. The doping control officer may then squat down and watch as you sit down because they need to be in full view of where the sample is coming from at all times. But what if I have to do number two? Well they will be right there with you, too. If you are a female and it is that time of the month you still need to use the restroom in front of that person while you change your sanitary products.

Once the sample has been collected, you pour your sample into bottles and then are asked to fill out a form. One thing that has gotten athletes in trouble in the past is the question, "Have you taken any medications?" Athletes frequently respond "no" even if they have. I am not sure if it is because they are ashamed to say they took something or they are confident that what they took is not prohibited. This is important because if you list a medication and are somehow found to have committed a violation because of that medication, the outcome of the decision could change based on whether or not you listed that medication on the form.

Supplements: Know what you are putting in your body. Some athletes go as far as having the products tested so that they see the exact ingredients. There is a downloadable Supplement Guide on the USADA website as well as a Supplement 411 page that will help you understand what to be aware of.

Recreational drugs: I am a square who has never tried a cigarette much less anything that would be considered a drug. However I am aware that other athletes choose to experiment with drugs such as cocaine and marijuana while they are not competing. Those drugs are banned in competition and it adds quite a bit of stress to your life to have to think about when you last used drug XYZ and when it will be out of your system. Wouldn't you hate to erase four years of waiting on a chance to compete on the Olympic stage because of a wild night out? It's not only about what is legal or illegal. Recreational drugs have the potential to enhance sports performance. Additionally, recreational drugs pose a potential health risk to the athlete and violate the spirit of sports.

Medication/TUE: In some situations, an athlete may have an illness or condition that requires the use of medication listed on the World Anti-Doping Agency's (WADA) prohibited list. You may be granted a Therapeutic Use Exemption (TUE) in these situations. The TUE application process is designed to provide athletes access to critical medication while protecting the rights of clean athletes to compete on a level playing field.

Who to contact: The USOC Athlete Ombudsman provides independent advice to athletes, at no cost. While you can contact the Ombudsman for various reasons, you should definitely reach out as a first step if you have a positive test. You will need legal help and this service is provided at no cost to you.

I really believe there is a misconception about how a lot of athletes test positive for banned substances. From my conversations with professional athletes over the years, it seems like many athletes who tested positive were not aware that what they were ingesting was banned. There is no doubt that there are athletes out there who are trying to gain an advantage, but drugs are everywhere and many average Joes are unknowing users or distributors.

My Story About Doping

I had three experiences where I was offered a quick fix. These were not back alley meetings and I didn't go seeking out drugs, or even supplements for that matter. However, the reality is that if you're an average Joe athlete or "weekend warrior" no one is testing you. And there are a lot more average Joes and weekend warriors than there are professional athletes. These products target the masses so you can find all sorts of ingredients in them. But we as professional athletes are held to a different standard and we have to have far more knowledge about these products than the general population.

In this world the more recognition you gain, the wider your circle of resources. The problem is that not all resources are ones you should use, and sifting through them becomes quite taxing. Plagued with nagging injuries over the years, at different times, I asked fellow elite athletes what they were doing to maintain their health. A few of my multimillion-dollar buddies had recommendations, but the lack of my own multimillion-dollar budget prevented me from ever following through, until a long talk with a friend led to me getting the hook up. "Go see my doc," he had said many times over the years. Now, I was finally getting my chance.

The picture he painted was that this guy was the "sports doctor of all sports doctors," well- versed in all aspects of what an athlete needs. With a five-year-old mystery hamstring ailment that produced shooting pains down my leg and occasional numbness and tingling in my feet, I was excited to meet him. Additionally, I felt I was not recovering quite the same lately and believed it was related to my menstrual cycle. My theory was that if I could just get some sort of advanced blood analysis that could tell me what to eat at a particular time of the month, it might make a difference.

I knew he provided supplements and that I would have to listen to why I should take them but that was not my focus. I have no problem hearing people out. If someone can logically explain to me how you get 37 servings of broccoli, 22 pounds of spinach and 7 pounds of asparagus into a single scoop of green powder, I might jump on the bandwagon. My problem with supplements is that they don't make sense. I understand I am not a scientist so some of the process is outside of my expertise, but it seems there should be a basic explanation that I can comprehend. When I run into these distributors no one can even begin to explain how these wonderful magic powders are produced, and that bothers me.

This "doctor" made his own supplements so I was optimistic that he could explain the process to me, but he couldn't. I thought, "Wait, you're the maker of this product and you can't tell me how it is made?" He began to get uneasy and I think I may have been the first person to ever ask him any detailed questions. But I kept going because I needed to know.

I was under the impression that he was medical doctor based on the way he was described to me, but he was actually a chiropractor. He had various certifications, which he described to me, but he emphasized his anti-aging certification. I was not knowledgeable enough at the time to know that should have been a red flag. Uninterested in that portion of his services anyway, I proceeded with various physical testing and analysis and ordered a blood and saliva test to conclude my visit.

A few days later, I described my visit to a medical doctor friend over breakfast and his response was to steer clear. He said, "We learn about these anti-aging guys in medical school. They are the latest snake oil salesmen." Now I was the one feeling uneasy.

A couple of weeks later the results of the test came in. I asked my doctor friend if he wouldn't mind listening in on the upcoming phone conversation to help me know what questions to ask and he agreed. He looked at my blood work before the call and said, "I guarantee this guy will tell you your hormone levels are all messed up. That is how anti-aging doctors make their money."

To summarize my phone conversation with the chiropractor, I had a food sensitivity to just about everything on the planet, high cholesterol, and my testosterone was low. I said, "I am a girl, I don't need high testosterone." He then told me that there was a ratio that I was well below and needed to increase. This is when the alarms started sounding in my head.

I asked, "So what can I eat to raise testosterone?"

He said, "You can't eat enough of anything to supplement that."

I joked, "Well there must be something I can eat to get the nutrition I need!"

He sounded frustrated and then suddenly said he was walking into a meeting and would have to call me back later. That was the last time we spoke. After we hung up, my doctor friend called me back and said, "This guy could be the next Balco scandal. Please put something in writing saying you decline his services and stay away from him."

I think the person who sent me to see this man had good intentions. I think the chiropractor distributing these products believes he is smarter than everyone else. The reality is that he found a professional sports organization (the NFL) with lax testing policies where the things he sells aren't tested for, so it was a great market to make big money. Then someone referred him to me, a track and field athlete, who is a member of a much more complex testing organization, paranoid about supplements, and not afraid to ask questions.

I dodged a bullet but still have a lot of regrets about this series of events. The main one is that I didn't hang up the phone and call USADA to report it. I guess I didn't see how it would matter at the time when the majority of his clients participated in other professional sports not regulated by USADA.

It is my belief that this same chiropractor cost someone very close to me his career. At first I felt a tremendous sense of guilt, but as time passes the guilt is subsiding. However, from that incident, I learned a very valuable lesson. Decision making gives you three options. You can do the right thing, do the wrong thing, or do nothing. Doing nothing can sometimes be the wrong thing, especially if it costs someone else their career.

I don't know everything, but I do know that educating athletes is the starting point. I am sure others have stories to tell and we need to hear them so we can have tangible examples of how these situations unfold. If you ever feel uncomfortable with something or someone you encounter, reach out to USADA immediately.

Imagine if I had inadvertently doped in the last year of my career when I was naturally slowing down. It would have looked like I was trying to get ahead of the system and cheating other athletes out of spots they had naturally won. It would have been the perfect storm, destroying my legacy.

At the time of writing this book, the chiropractor "doctor" is still out there taking advantage of athletes and football players. A track and field athlete could end up in his hands again. That scares me.

Believe in yourself and invest the time and money necessary to have good nutrition. Use nothing unless prescribed by a medical doctor for medical purposes, and even then, explain to them that you are in a testing program and you need to check with USADA before taking what they prescribe for you.

CHAPTER 9

TRAVEL

---

*"Put your competition gear and your competition shoes
in your carry-on luggage every time you travel. No
exceptions! You do not want to be faced with missing an
opportunity to perform because of lost luggage."*

-Lauryn Williams

As a professional athlete you will get to travel all over the world. Many will tell you how lucky you are. They are right. You are lucky to get to see and experience the world in all of its beauty, and do most of it on someone else's dime.

There are some untold parts of a professional athlete's travel life that are far less glamorous. In some countries you will only see the airport, hotel, and track. There may be times you take a red eye flight, get off the plane, and go compete. Sitting in a cramped economy seat for 10+ hours next to a screaming sick baby is not conducive to getting much rest. I know from experience that traveling can be exhausting. I want to give you some valuable tips I have learned that will help you minimize the potential pitfalls of traveling abroad.

Understanding the Calendar Year

Get a good understanding of how your season works. Track and field athletes start around October with fall training. January through March is indoor season. March through May is what I like to call pre-season. May through August is competition season, although September and possibly even October could have competitions. Overall, people will start to shut it down in late August and take the month of September off. There will be some travel outside of the country prior to the USA championships in June, but generally once your USATF championships are done in June you will head over to Europe for the remainder of the summer because that is where most of the opportunities are to compete.

Being Sick While Traveling

Being ill is never fun. Getting ill in a country outside of your own is even less fun. What if you get sick and you don't know what medicine to take because the label is in a different language? Now you have a potential anti-doping problem on your hands. Pack a small medical kit of common things you know are approved to take for a stomach ache, headache, or virus. Also take an anti-itch cream, Neosporin or other antibacterial cream for cuts, Bandaids, electrolytes, eye drops, and insect repellent.

You should also find out what the equivalent to 9-1-1 is, because 9-1-1 is not the emergency number worldwide.

Being a Considerate Traveler

Sometimes as Americans we expect the rest of the world to be able to speak English in addition to their native tongue. Remember that you are in a different country and try not to be frustrated if very few people speak English. How many different languages do you know? Using Google Translate or a different app on your phone can be your best friend when there is no one in sight who speaks English. There are also apps that allow you to use the camera on your phone to take a picture of a sign, menu, food label, etc., and it will translate the text for you into English.

Besides the language, the food, brands in the store, transportation, and customs (like what side of the sidewalk you should walk on) might be very different from what you're used to. Try not to complain loudly in public about cultural differences. You're not just a representation of your sponsor's brand or the sport you compete in, you're actually a representation of Americans. Certain European countries do not look fondly on Americans, and if you are rude and loud this could only add fuel to the fire.

When Traveling By Car

Be careful when taking taxis and cars. You can end up in the wrong place because you got in a car with a driver who doesn't speak English; you used the one word in their language that you knew, and they nodded their head and took off. It is good to have a business card or note on your phone with the address of your intended destination you can show them. When driving to local track meets, be mindful of the effect sitting in a car for hours can have on your body.

When Traveling By Plane

Be sure to sign up for every award program with every airline so that you earn miles and status when traveling. Your miles and status will carry you through your career and provide free off-season trips for you and your family. Upgrades on long flights are more affordable when you have status and can use miles. Most airlines have free upgrades for their frequent fliers with elite status.

You can stay connected on flights in different ways, too. For example, T-Mobile gives you one hour of free wi-fi on flights that use gogoinflight as their provider. Other times your upgrade or airline status will give you free wi-fi.

Here is some advice for airports in general. Paying extra to have TSA PreCheck and Global Entry will save you time and stress in travel. If you have TSA PreCheck you'll go through a separate security line once you check in, and you won't have to take off your shoes, belt, or light jacket and you won't have to remove your laptop or 3-1-1 compliant liquids from your carry-on bag on the conveyor belt. If you have Global Entry you'll skip the long customs lines when you come back into America and go straight to a special kiosk.

Consider where you are traveling, and how long the security lines may be when you are thinking about what time to arrive at the airport. If you are checking a bag, you will be required to be there earlier than if you are not checking a bag. I have been burnt many times for leaving the house at my usual time, then realizing that it was too late to check my bag. If it is an international flight, you will need to check in earlier than if it is a domestic flight in the USA. Also, when traveling internationally, know that each airline and each country has their own rules. While arriving at the airport two to three hours in advance is a suggestion, there are a few airlines that require you to be at the airport two hours in advance.

Something else to consider is the chance you may be randomly selected for an extra security check. If you see the letters SSSS on your boarding pass, TSA will be taking you aside to go through the contents of your carry-on. This can happen to anyone regardless of their status.

Remember to budget for baggage. If you don't have status with the airline you are flying with, expect to pay to check your luggage. When you are traveling abroad be mindful that European carriers are super strict with both carry-on and checked bags, weighing them and putting them in bins to make sure they are not oversized. If they are overweight or oversized, you could be charged extra fees.

If you are a field event person, your implements need to get to your destination. Pole vault poles do not fit on all planes. Your stuff may have to take a different route than you. Get familiar with how to best travel with your equipment and ask other athletes in your event how they travel with their stuff. Be sure to label your equipment and luggage inside and out with your name and contact information, so that if they are lost, the airline will be able to get in touch with you. Make friends with the employees at your home airport in case you ever need their help.

Be kind and respectful to the gate agents who can grant you different seats and allow you to potentially get on the plane you arrived late to check in for. Don't act like you deserve to be treated like royalty and expect to get an upgrade or receive a favor from them. Kill them with kindness and they may help you instead of putting you in a middle seat that doesn't recline by the bathroom.

YES, THAT HAPPENED!

In London's Heathrow Airport, I was catching a connecting flight and needed to get a new boarding pass. My plane had landed for a three-hour layover. I walked forty-five minutes through the airport to reach the line for a boarding pass. When I reached the front of the line, the woman said, "Check-in is two hours before the flight." I replied, "I walked forty-five minutes and stood in this line for the boarding pass. There are still two hours left." She said, "Ma'am, it's an hour and fifty-nine minutes before your flight." I was flabbergasted.

In that situation, she did not check me in. She would not give me a boarding pass despite the fact that the next available flight I could take was not until the next day. I had to walk to a nearby hotel dragging my luggage and navigating confusing signs. I slept for a few hours and then returned to the airport with plenty of time before my morning flight to make sure there was no confusion. I ended up getting to Morocco on the day of the race, missing lunch and any time to connect with other athletes. I had to convince the host to find something for me to eat, with only three hours left before my race.

This stuff really happens! I lost the race.

Lauryn Williams

Some airports are not fun to travel through. It is unfortunate but true. You will have to walk what feels like five miles from one terminal to the next, the customer service will be poor, and there will be limited food options. One of my dream jobs is to be an airport efficiency consultant. I feel like they never consult with those who travel frequently.

As a professional it is your job to prepare for this and not let travel inefficiencies drain your energy. Prepare for the worst and hope for the best. I try to avoid certain airports at all costs now. However, if I have to fly through one of them I come prepared because at the end of the day I am in charge of my attitude and they cannot steal my joy.

Once you arrive at your destination in the foreign country's airport, you will go through customs and collect your luggage. Going through customs is a serious matter. Customs is not the place to be loudly cracking jokes or taking pictures (which are normally forbidden). The more you travel the more accustomed you will become to the various cultures. Some countries are stricter than others. You will have to fill out a form that they give you on the plane answering questions about what the purpose is for your visit and the address where you will be staying. Then you will stand in line to be interviewed before they stamp your passport and let you into the country.

Be prepared to answer questions like, "What is the purpose of your trip? Are you going to make money while you are here? Have you filled out any tax forms for those earnings? Where are you staying?" Responding with a sassy attitude is a terrible idea. Some places are known for being hard on Americans and could take you aside to question you more.

YES, THAT HAPPENED!

I traveled to London my first year as a pro athlete and didn't know much about international travel. When I arrived, everyone was herded off the plane and into lines. I had no clue what was going on. I got in line (or queue) and finally made it to the front. A man instructed me to go to a customs agent. As I made my way to her, I put on my best smile and said "hello" in an upbeat tone. She asked for my passport and I gave it to her. She asked me how many days I was staying in London and I told her three.

Then things got serious.

She asked, "Where are you staying?"

I replied, "I don't know."

She asked, "Who is picking you up?"

I said, "I don't know."

She asked, "Why are you here?"

I said, "For a track meet."

She asked, "What's that?"

I thought, "Who doesn't know what track meet is?"

She said, "Are you an athlete?"

I said, "Yes."

She said, "So you do athletics?"

I had no clue what that was. I said, "No I run track."

She asked me for a contact number for someone in the country.

I told her, "I don't know anyone here."

Then she told me a long story about her trip to California and how they detained her because she had written something down wrong. I replied and said, "Okay, what does that have to do with me?" She sent me to the back. Let's just say you don't want to go to the back. I stayed there for a while until Coach Amy Deem and JB from the track meet came and saved me.

Wallace Spearmon Jr.
Two-time Olympian

Travel Food

Proper nutrition is key to success in our sport. There is a lot you cannot control when traveling by plane like the weather, mechanical delays, and traffic control stops. What you thought would be a quick trip could turn into a long journey with not enough time to buy food in the airport during your layover before your next flight. You may have to miss a meal from time to time for one reason or another. You will be best prepared if you train yourself to always pack a bunch of snacks. And not just any snacks, healthy snacks. Filling up with junk food won't be helpful for your performance as an athlete now, or for your body later.

Here are a few of the items I made sure I packed when I traveled to compete:

- Nuts
- Bars
- Jerky
- Granola

- Trail mix
- Rice cakes
- Oatmeal (easy to add hot water just about anywhere)
- Peanut butter
- Jelly
- Hot sauce (this is a game changer for a bland meal)

One of the biggest adjustments a new athlete has when they travel is learning what and how to eat in foreign countries. Picky eaters will have a very tough time. It is not ideal to eat fast food every day. Rice and pasta can become your best friend and worst enemy. Meets often provide the meals and you should be prepared to eat what is traditional in that country.

At some meets, you'll find that adequate or proper meals are not provided prior to competitions. Others will have a large variety of things to choose from but you may not have eaten many of the things offered before. Deciding to eat out every night could add up. Consider your budget and your body's needs before you spend money on food. Is what is being offered going to prohibit you from getting proper nutrition to compete or are you just being a prima donna?

TRAVELING WITH A SPOUSE

My wife is not an athlete and was never around anything related to sports. She knew I jumped well, but didn't fully know what being a professional meant. One year when I was at a competition in Europe, she decided to come. She thought it would be fun to take a class and spend time with me. Until this point, neither of us realized that when I am in competitive mode, I am emotionally unavailable.

This trip was difficult. It put a strain on our relationship. A lot of Olympians are challenged with this. You have to have focus and continually perfect your skill and it can be hard for people close to you to have insight into that if they're not an athlete. The people who know us best usually have no idea what our professional lives are like. It's awesome when someone can support you through the intense times, but you won't always be able to support them in ways they would like you to when you are under pressure.

Matt Hemmingway
Olympic Silver Medalist, High Jump

Other Travel Tips

- Pack for all types of weather and dress in layers on the plane. Planes can be cold even though you are traveling to a warm destination. Spending the "summer" in Europe may have you thinking you should only pack summer clothes, but their summer highs could feel like springtime temperatures to you. Research the average annual temperatures and the upcoming forecast before you pack.

- Be mindful of the various perspectives and political environments in foreign countries, as some people can be very intolerant of Americans.

- When you are in a foreign country, don't assume people don't understand English. Just because someone doesn't speak it, doesn't mean they don't understand what you are saying.

- Do not rely on electronics and technology working in a foreign country. If you get off the plane and you have no phone service or your battery has died and you don't have a converter to charge it, you could be in deep trouble. Research international phone/data plans and voltage and outlets in the country you'll be traveling to so you can be prepared.

- Know the name of your hotel and a contact person. Have a copy of that information and your hotel reservation printed out in case you aren't able to access it with your phone. When you get to the hotel, take their business card with you so you can show someone where you are trying to go if you get lost.

- Don't forget to sign up for hotel rewards.

- Don't be a target. Walking around in the full USA gear is not ideal. The perception in some places is that Americans have iPhones and cash.

- Ice is a luxury in many foreign countries. Make friends with the hotel staff if you are hoping to get an ice bath during your stay.

You will spend a lot of time on the road. Make sure you have something to do during your down time. This is a great time to invest in yourself via blogs, podcasts, e-books, or online learning. While Netflix is addictingly entertaining, binge watching shows is not the most productive use of your time.

If you are not accustomed to traveling by yourself, find comfort in knowing that elite athletes typically have similar international itineraries. The same people you competed against last week will likely be the same ones you see next week. A race may be happening in France one week and Italy the next, but the faces don't change much. As you travel more, even when your main buddies are not around you will find comfort in seeing familiar faces, and it will only be a matter of time before you'll see your travel buddies again.

YES, THAT HAPPENED!

One of my first international trips was to Brazil in 2010. I had several stops before reaching my destination. I should have asked some questions about what to do in the travel process before I left. I landed in Brazil and was led to baggage claim. What I didn't realize was that I was supposed to grab my bags and transfer them to the next flight. I thought the trip was over. In 2010 international cell phones were not the norm, but I finally found a way to reach my agent. By the time he told me I had another connecting flight, it was too late to catch it, so he had to rebook my flight. The meet organizers were beyond angry because they had a busload of people waiting for me to arrive before they could depart for a long ride to the hotel. It was a mess. Half a day later, I got to where I was supposed to be. Lord only knows the charges incurred to get me there.

Amber Campbell
Three-time Olympian

CHAPTER 10

MORE THAN JUST AN ATHLETE

"Running professionally was one of the greatest experiences of my life. There is something so pure and freeing about giving everything you have to be great at something. That being said, it doesn't last forever and one must always be planning an exit strategy."

-Nick Symmonds, two-time Olympian, CEO of Run Gum

Who are you besides an athlete? Get out a piece of paper right now and list three roles you play in the world without listing athlete as one. Think about all the things you are: someone's child, a spouse, a parent, a sibling, an American, a finance major, a House of Cards fanatic, a rubix cube magician, an artist, or a musician. You are more than what the clock or measuring tape says you are.

Competing in sports offers amazing experiences and helps to shape who you are, but *sport is what you do, not who you are.* When your confidence and identity come from being an athlete, everything can be ripped away suddenly. Without real purpose outside of sport, you might find yourself at the peak of your career, injured, and feeling lost.

There are three things that can help you to learn who you are and remember that you are more than just an athlete: understanding the experiences of your past, making the most of the present, and looking forward to your future after competing.

Understanding the Experiences of Your Past

Your past is made up of tons of experiences, both good and bad. Your life hasn't always been about just being an athlete. You may have played the starring role in the school play, took a family vacation that you'll never forget, or graduated at the top of your class. You probably had plenty of activities that you enjoyed doing and people that you liked spending time with.

Even though those things are in the past, it's important to embrace them and cherish them. They helped to make you who you are, not only as an athlete but as a person. And, sometimes it's these good memories that you hold onto that will help you get through difficult and challenging times in the present and future.

Now, there are probably some painful experiences from your past as well. Everyone has them. It's important that you acknowledge these parts of your life also. You might have grown up abused, fatherless, bullied, compared to others, poor, and never praised. You cannot alter your past story. The unpleasant things from your past are part of who you are just as much as the good memories that you hold.

If you think you can push those things into the closet and just focus on your life of building your career as an athlete and move on to better times you are wrong! You will feel like an imposter, and at some point, you will decide you can no longer hide the other parts of who you are. The moment you decide to no longer hide is the moment you begin to identify with yourself.

Olympic bronze medalist Kelly Wells overcame an abusive situation at home and was able to deal with pressure and tense situations a lot better because of her experience. She shares openly about this part of her story and doesn't try to hide her past. Once you've overcome something and received inner healing, there should be no shame attached to sharing your story publicly. In fact, it may give others hope and a way out of their own similar situations as well.

Remember that as a professional athlete, you have a platform that many others will never have. Kelly has been able to share her personal story and help others not just as an athlete, but as a real person that has been through real situations.

Just because you are now an athlete doesn't mean the other parts of your past vanish. These unhealed areas of our lives are where unwanted habits come from, such as excessive drinking or obsessive behavior. Take the time to face the events that have left you broken and shattered, otherwise the pain and anger will manifest in the worst possible moment.

We are not at our best when we are isolated. Mental health is not something you have to figure out on your own. Sports psychology is an underused resource, but it is a worthwhile investment in having a long career. And remember, you don't have to be mentally ill to be mentally unhealthy.

Our minds are powerful. Putting on a facade is exhausting. You may have experienced childhood tragedy, trauma, or abuse that not many know about. You also may have created a strong persona as a result. And maybe you don't want to acknowledge the demons that still haunt you. Un-dealt with negative self-talk and events from your past can destroy your ability to compete, but even worse, can destroy your life. The sooner you commit to being authentically you and get some inner healing, the sooner you can be free to compete without strongholds. Your own adversity will become your superpower strength!

Knowing and accepting who you were before you were an athlete, both the good and the bad, can help you to stay grounded and know who you are in the present and the future.

Making the Most of the Present

Being a professional athlete is a full-time commitment, so it's easy to fall into the trap of thinking that your every waking moment needs to be dedicated to your performance. When this happens your identity becomes wrapped up into who you are as an athlete instead of being grounded in who you are as a person. Your confidence soars with every first-place finish and disappears with a less than stellar performance. But, that's normal because you're a professional athlete, right?

Wrong! You may be tempted to wrap your identity inside your performance, but it is one of the most dangerous things you can do. Being your "best you" is a lifelong practice. You are an athlete, but that is not your entire makeup. Your participation in sports is part of your story, not the entire story. The biggest benefit of being an athlete is not money or medals, but building community, creating lifelong friendships, and having new experiences.

We push ourselves to reach perfection in sports and often don't stop until we get there. Don't let your aspiration ruin your relationships, which are far more valuable than medals and money. Your life is more than sports, even if it is the way you earn money. Don't forget to enjoy what is happening right now each and every day as you train.

One of the best things you can do to remind yourself that you are more than an athlete in the present is to spend time understanding and developing who you are outside of sports. As you discover your interests you will find great pleasure from life off the track. You could take time to expand your education, serve in an internship, or volunteer for an organization. Try out hobbies and explore what passions you have outside of your sport. It doesn't have to be grand; all of it matters.

Don't let others convince you that you're not focused enough because you have other interests. There's nothing wrong with being smart and furthering your education. And, there's nothing wrong with acknowledging your dreams and aspirations outside of sports.

While competing I got a masters degree in business, a real estate license, and took numerous Spanish and sign language classes. Taking time to do the things I was interested in was a welcome distraction from competing so that I was not obsessing over what didn't go well in practice or spending my time doing things that would hinder my performance. To learn sign language I volunteered at a school in a deaf classroom. Hanging out with the children was very rewarding. It reminded me of the importance of giving back while giving me a cool opportunity to learn to sign.

We talked about painful parts of your past but it is important to acknowledge that every day will not be wonderful in the present. There may be times where you find yourself at a low point in life and the athlete in you says, "I will gut this out." This seems like a good idea because as an athlete you are used to having to overcome obstacles in order to win, but not properly dealing with physical and emotional pain as it happens will take a bigger toll on you than you think. Your performance will suffer if you don't deal with life. If you take care of yourself, you will come back stronger and with more purpose. Here are some examples of how to heal in the present from situations frequently encountered:

- If someone close to you passes away it is important to take time to grieve. Bottling up your emotions might make it look like you are doing okay, but all those emotions will build up and eventually impact all areas of your life.

- If you are injured, do not be afraid to rest and pull back partially or fully from training and competing. You can make things worse and depending on the severity, end your season or career by trying to be tough.

- If you break up with your significant other, embrace the hurt and surround yourself with family and friends who love you unconditionally. You may need counseling to process the inner turmoil.

There's nothing wrong with taking time to heal.

In the present, continue to enjoy the other areas of your life. Laugh with your friends, take a cooking class, develop the business plan for that idea you've always had in the back of your mind. And, I think you'll find that when you put your life in balance, you will excel more in all areas and find that you enjoy competing even more.

Looking Forward to the Future

The biggest pitfall that many athletes face sneaks up on all of us; it's the feeling that we are invincible. Even though you are just beginning your career as a professional track and field athlete it's important that you keep in mind there will be an end. The illusion of immortality causes many to forsake preparation for the future. But, the day comes for every single athlete when it's time to move on.

You want to prepare yourself mentally, emotionally, and financially for the day when that transition happens. But, remember that it still doesn't mean it's going to be easy. When my career as a professional athlete came to an end I had money in savings, two degrees, multiple certificates in various things, didn't need to immediately look for work, yet the transition was still tough. When so much of your life has been focused in one area for so long it's unrealistic to think that leaving it behind is going to be a breeze.

When you get to this point of your career remind yourself that it's okay to mourn that your time as a professional athlete is over. That's actually normal for people when they retire from a career, not just athletes. You may even find yourself having to work through the five stages of grief:

1. Denial: "I didn't really have to stop competing. I should still be on the team."

2. Anger: "If [fill in the blank] didn't happen I would still be able to continue competing for longer."

3. Bargaining: "Maybe if I work really hard I can get back in for just one more year."

4. Depression: "I have nothing now that my career is over. I'm worthless outside of my sport."

5. Acceptance: "There is more to life than sports. I can now spend time [fill in the blank]."

There are still days when I go back to the bargaining phase. When I was trying to decide what life after sports activity was right for me, I wanted to choose something that would have a lasting impact. I had no idea how it would turn out, but I took a leap of faith and started my financial business in order to serve others.

When we focus on our own comfort, goals, or hopes alone, we lose sight of our bigger purpose. For me that purpose is using my talents to honor God and serve people well.

If you deal with the past and invest in yourself in yourself now, your transition to the future is going to be much smoother because you'll be more prepared for life after sports. It's okay to not know exactly what you want to do when your career comes to an end, but if you've been investing time into connecting with your greater purpose, you won't feel completely lost when your career has come to an end.

PRO TIP 👍 TRAIN YOUR THINKING PATTERNS

Focus on what you want instead of what you don't want. Thinking, "I am going to stop doing this," or "I am not going to do that" is not productive because you are inadvertently bringing the thing you are trying to eliminate to the front of your mind. Instead focus on the things you want like, "I want to run the fastest rep in practice today." Or, "I am going to jump farther than the mark in the sand."

When we don't perform well we can either bounce back or let it overcome us. Avoid negative self-talk. Would you say those things to a child? Being self-critical is unproductive. Be kind to yourself.

We are not at our best when we are isolated. Mental health is not something you have to figure out on your own. Sports psychology is an underused resource, but it is a worthwhile investment in having a long career.

CHAPTER 11

REPRESENTING YOUR COUNTRY

"I've been lucky enough to witness the concept of team as a Team USA member at the Olympics and at the IAAF World Championships. The positive energy you absorb from others in a team event, or in training, is no doubt the most uplifting force you've ever experienced. The enthusiasm of the coaches/managers, the support of the medical staff, and the camaraderie all add up to a team of like-minded individuals who share in the same quest: to be the best team ever assembled."

-Bernard Lagat, two-time Olympian

We have made it to the end! This book has given you the tools to help you excel as a professional track and field athlete. I have no doubt that you are better equipped to maximize your potential and make the most of your time as a professional track and field athlete. I hope you make the team and get to stand on the podium.

My goal was to give you vision at the beginning of your professional career of where you could end up: on the U.S. National Team. This is a huge accomplishment and there are so many people who have worked their entire lives to get to this point. Don't take it lightly.

Remember, there is no "I" in Team. When you put on that uniform you are a member of Team USA first and foremost. Here are some tips for you about how to represent your country well.

FAN TIP 👍

Rooting *for* your team doesn't mean rooting *against* a competitor. Be gracious. Be a good sport. Show some class. "USA! USA! USA!" is appropriate. "You couldn't outrun my momma you ugly hippopotamus!" is not appropriate.

Stars on the Right, Stripes on the Left: I have been to four Olympic Games and a bunch of World Championships where I have earned medals. Yet, a quick Google search will yield only one picture of me holding the American flag...the wrong way! In the excitement of the moment, please remember that your right hand should be on the stars and your left hand on the stripes. Learn from me and don't make the same mistake.

You Are Already a Winner: You have already won! Of course, your aspiration is to be on top of the podium, but being on top of the podium is not the only kind of winning. Trying your best and competing with integrity are the things you already conquered to get to this point. These are the things that make you a winner, not a medal. Only a fraction of a percent of the people in the world will achieve this honor. Think about that for a minute. You are one of the greats! This is a once in a lifetime journey for most and an accomplishment the majority of people will never experience. Be proud of yourself and enjoy the gravity of the moment; it may not come again.

Dare To Be the Same: Don't make the mistake of trying to change things up for a championship race. You don't need a miracle, magic, or divine intervention to do well at the Olympics or IAAF World Championships. You don't need to "dare to be different." Instead, dare to be the same. All you need to do is the same thing you did to reach this point. Do the same thing at the Games that you do any time you compete, just with more focus, less distraction, and more confidence.

Good Team Chemistry Is Important: Many Olympic athletes are placed in a situation that can be hard to balance. Your Team USA teammates may also be your competition. And, not just your former competition outside of the Olympics, but the people you are competing against for that coveted gold medal. So, now you have the challenge of learning how to build camaraderie with people as you also compete against them. Remember that we are stronger together. Team USA is the best team in the world. Prioritize compassion and professionalism over winning and you will surely be satisfied with the result.

Communicate Clearly With Your Support System: A strong support system is a great thing to have. However, make sure that you don't let your support system become a distraction to you. You are the only person who will know best what you need at each moment. Clearly communicate these needs to your coach, agent, family, and friends so they know what you need from them. Communicate early and often; do not wait until you have reached the point of frustration before you speak up. Your support system wants to see you do well and will understand if you need some silence and solitude. There will be plenty of things that can keep them busy while you focus on preparing for your performance. You have worked hard to get to this point so don't worry about being selfish with how you spend your time in order to perform at your best.

Take Time To Learn From Others: You are getting ready to meet people from all over the world. Take time to chat with other athletes who are pursuing their dreams as well. Get to know them. Iron sharpens iron, and there is a lot that you can learn from the other athletes you meet during the Games. Learning about different cultures and perspectives will help you grow as a person and as an athlete. Keep an open heart and an open mind during your journey.

Take It All In: Don't forget to take a moment to soak it all in. Live in the moment. Please, make sure you step back for a moment to observe where your hard work has gotten you. Take in the sights, sounds, and smells. Enjoy living in the moment, if even for just a minute. It is a moment you will never forget. Let gratitude be your guide and you won't go home regretting your result. Enjoy your journey! I will be watching and cheering!

CHAPTER 12

BONUS CHAPTER:
RELAYS

"Caution. Objects may be closer than they appear. At the end of the day nothing should come between you and your teammates. When you let outside forces in, bad things happen."

-Wallace Spearmon Jr., two-time Olympian

This chapter does not apply to most track and field athletes, but I would be remiss to not add some advice and perspective on relays. Relays can be a political and gray area as well as a subjective process. Much of the drama surrounding relays is related to unrealistic expectations. Let me see if I can explain.

Relays are not usually an athlete's aspiration when they envision making the team. Not too many people grow up saying they want to be a professional relay runner. While there are various relays to add excitement to the sport, I want to focus on the two that are a part of the official IAAF program: the 4 X 1 relay or the 4 X 4 relay. Generally, you're a 100-meter runner or a 400-meter runner when you run relays. Each year your goal is to make the IAAF World Championships or Olympic team in your individual event. If you meet that goal, you are added to the relay pool and you could have an opportunity to compete. It is not a given.

Even though four people compete in the relay, usually the top six to eight athletes are in a pool and coaches move you around to make sure your chemistry is good. Let's say you get 5th or 6th at the USA Championships and you've been selected for the relay pool. You didn't really do your job because you did not finish top three in your open event. Being selected for the relay pool is a second tier saving grace. The top four finishers at USA Championships are given an automatic bid to be a part of the relay pool. The coach then gets to make two discretionary picks taking the total to six. Some coaches choose their athletes who didn't make the finals of their event. In fact, anyone officially named to that year's team roster is eligible to participate in the relay, even a thrower. But wait it gets more convoluted.

Once those picks are made, the athletes are invited to participate in a training camp usually held in Monaco, where two more athletes are invited to work with the team. So now there are eight. These spots are intended for two people who want to come and get some extra "experience" in case they are chosen at some point in the future. Now, sometimes those invited for experience have participated and ended up replacing one of the six originally named. And last but not least the coach invites two more athletes to be alternates to the alternates, just in case someone gets hurt. So there are sometimes ten people for six spots. This selection process is considered standard for Team USA relays.

Once training camp is over the ten drops to eight. Practices are held at the championships where the coach is supposed to drop the number to six, the final number of athletes to participate in the prelims and finals. This is where the chaos is amplified. During practices you see coaches, agents, training partners, priests, shoe company reps, and sometimes campaign managers lobbying for their athlete to be part of the relay. If you have a good coach who does a good job of managing team chemistry, the team will be on the same page and won't pay attention to outside distractions. But what typically happens is that no one knows the order of the relay, who is running, or if they are even in the pool until the day of the race. When the team is managed in this manner the result is usually a baton rolling across the track and four people walking to the finish line instead of running.

Relays are hard enough to figure out without adding unnecessary drama to the mix. So, if you are chosen, be grateful for it and do everything you can to help the team win. To demonstrate, I will rehash one of my very dramatic relay experiences.

was on a relay team and the fastest runner was calling the shots. You can see how that might be problem.) The coaches went out of their way to accommodate her wishes. She wanted to run anchor leg so she could run across the finish line for publicity purposes. Well, in the 4x1 relay the hand-off (who holds the baton in what hand) goes right, left, right, left. The first athlete runs with the baton in the right hand so they can be on the inside of the lane when the baton is passed (in order to cover the shortest amount of distance in the race). As a basic principle the first runner should be comfortable holding a baton in his/her right hand.

Well, she wanted it left, right, left, right. Doing things the opposite way than they are traditionally done for your own comfort is crazy inefficient and a ticking time bomb! On top of that, making your three teammates uncomfortable is selfish. If you can't take the baton in your proper hand, there is no place for you in the relay.

Obviously, coaching could have been better in this instance. A good relay coach doesn't care if you are No. 1 in the world. Chemistry should reign supreme. Relay is a team effort and no one person should have total control. We're Team USA. Our top eight in the country could easily be top ten in the world. We have seen others demonstrate you don't have to be the fastest to win.

She had won the USA Championship but I had won the IAAF World Championships. I took advantage of my higher success and changed the relay back to normal handoffs. We only had a couple of days to practice. We won the race and things turned out fine, however, the entire ordeal was stressful for the team.

The relay is a team effort. When you get the privilege to join forces with other members of Team USA, make it an enjoyable experience. Put the team before your own desires and communicate clearly. Remember that your value to the team is not only in how well you do on the track. Your role as a supportive teammate is a very important contribution.

ENCOURAGING SCRIPTURES

As a Christian athlete, I receive great joy, wisdom, and help from reading the Bible. There are many Bible verses that have encouraged me both in everyday life and in training to compete. Here is a list of some of my favorite verses.

> I have fought the good fight,
> I have finished the race,
> I have kept the faith.
> *2 Timothy 4:7 NKJV*

> Therefore we also, since we are surrounded by so great a
> cloud of witnesses, let us lay aside every weight,
> and the sin which so easily ensnares us, and let us run
> with endurance the race that is set before us,
> looking unto Jesus, the author and finisher of our faith,
> who for the joy that was set before Him endured the cross,
> despising the shame, and has sat down at the right
> hand of the throne of God.
> *Hebrews 12:1-2 NKJV*

For physical training is of some value, but godliness has value for all things, holding promise for both the present life and the life to come.
1 Timothy 4:8 NIV

But those who wait on the Lord
Shall renew their strength;
They shall mount up with wings like eagles,
They shall run and not be weary,
They shall walk and not faint.
Isaiah 40:31 NKJV

For physical training is of some value, but godliness has value for all things, holding promise for both the present life and the life to come.
1 Timothy 4:8 NIV

I [Jesus] have come that they may have life, and that they may have it more abundantly.
John 10:10 NKJV

I press on to take hold of that for which Christ Jesus took hold of me. Brothers and sisters, I do not consider myself yet to have taken hold of it. But one thing I do: Forgetting what is behind and straining toward what is ahead, I press on toward the goal to win the prize for which God has called me heavenward in Christ Jesus.
Philippians 3:12-14 NIV

THE FINISH LINE

————

While there is more information for you to discover in the journey of becoming a professional athlete, I hope the pages of this book have provided you with some foundational materials to move forward in the pursuit of your dreams. This endeavor may seem overwhelming, but do not quit.

I have compiled many resources as well as all the links in the book for your convenience. Check them out at *the-oval-office.com*

Pursuing your dreams is worth all the effort it will take to achieve your goals. Life is a marathon and not a sprint. Fix your eyes on the finish line and go for the gold!

ABOUT THE AUTHOR

Lauryn Williams is an Olympic sprinter and bobsledder. In her 12 years of competing at the highest level, she's won countless accolades and competed in over 20 countries. During the four Olympic Games she attended, Lauryn earned one gold and two silver medals. She is also the first American woman to earn medals in both the Summer and Winter Olympic Games.

She has been featured in Sports Illustrated, the LA Times, CBS, Money magazine, Muse magazine, the Bleacher Report, Investment News "40 under 40," and more. Lauryn has been invited to speak in front of the U.S. congress, at various Women's Sports Foundation events, the WADA symposium, to NFL draft participants, and at the USATF annual meeting.

During her time as an athlete, Lauryn pursued an education in Finance and Business earning a BA and an MBA in those fields, respectively.

In 2015, after retiring from competing, she turned her attention to working as a financial planner and educator opening her own financial planner and educator and opened her own financial company called "Worth Winning." Lauryn helps clients, many of whom are athletes like herself, optimize their finances, careers, and their future.

She is a staunch supporter of community building and giving back.

She offers her time and knowledge to many organizations including The Junior League, USATF Athletes Advisory Committee, USADA, and WADA.

An avid home chef, Lauryn loves spending time in the kitchen preparing healthy meals with her great dane, Yasu, by her side.

If you have questions for Lauryn regarding becoming a professional athlete, or if you are looking for additional resources, go to *Lauryn-Williams.com.*

For more information on financial planning, including free resources, visit *Worth-Winning.com.*

Made in the USA
Las Vegas, NV
23 October 2023

79608233R00092